Rising

Rising

The Amazing Story of Christianity's Resurrection in the Global South

Dyron B. Daughrity

Fortress Press
Minneapolis

This book is dedicated to the missionaries, martyrs, converts, and countless others who preserved the Christian faith despite many difficulties and at times severe persecution. Due to their resilience and tenacity, Christianity is rising.

With profound respect, the author of this volume would like to pay special tribute to the Christians of China and Russia during the twentieth century, especially those who presented the ultimate sacrifice to their Lord and Savior Jesus Christ.

Contents

Acknowledgments

First, I must acknowledge the excellent editorial work of Lisa Kloskin at Fortress Press. It was my privilege to be chosen by her to write for Fortress Press, and she worked most efficiently to keep the book on track. Thank you, Lisa. It is a pleasure to work with you.

I extend a sincere thanks to my colleagues at Pepperdine. They continue to offer me encouragement at every turn. A special word of thanks goes to professors Tim Willis and Dan Rodriguez for their salutary leadership in our division.

I acknowledge my wonderful students, especially those with whom I have worked personally. I must single out my graduate assistant Mike Gaston for helping me with various tasks as I worked on this book.

I gratefully acknowledge the loving support of my wife, Sunde, and our four children: Clare Soleil, Ross Dyron, Mande Mae, and Holly Joy. It was a difficult year in many ways, especially after my facial injury and surgery. You have been gracious and patient as we packed up in preparation for our move to Italy. Thank you for your unfailing love and unconditional acceptance.

I am also most grateful to my loving parents, May Dell and Jerald Daughrity. It was such a blessing to celebrate your fiftieth wedding anniversary with you on 8 August 2017.

And finally, as always, I humbly acknowledge Jesus Christ, my Lord:

Now unto him that is able to do exceeding abundantly above all that we ask or think, according to the power that worketh in us, Unto him be glory in the church by Christ Jesus throughout all ages, world without end. Amen. (Ephesians 3:20–21 KJV)

Dyron B. Daughrity
Florence, Italy
15 September 2017

Introduction

Port Dickson, Malaysia, is an odd place for someone to begin their life's work. I had gone there in 2004 to attend a conference on world missions. Between sessions, we were taken on a little outing to an old Christian cemetery. While walking around, looking at the graves of British and Canadian missionaries, it hit home that these individuals gave their lives for something greater than themselves. They came way out here to this little coastal town to bring the gospel. And now their remains were completely abandoned and alone, ignored by everyone, except for perhaps those engaged in a world missions conference.

I wondered how these individuals felt, moving their families way out here to a peninsula extending out from Southeast Asia. What motivated them to do something so radical? Their journey took place before air travel. It would have taken them months to get here by ship.

History shows that most missionaries accomplished little when measured by the number of people they converted to

Christianity. Many of them died shortly after their arrival because of their lack of immunity to new bacteria and viruses, especially in tropical environments. In the mission field, young children and mothers giving birth were especially vulnerable.

I stood in that cemetery wondering why these missionaries gave everything to bring the gospel to people they knew nothing about. Their dedication was obvious, but what motivated them? And where can this level of commitment possibly be found today?

As I was deep in thought, somebody tapped me on the shoulder. "Are you Dyron Daughrity?" Yes. Handing me a cell phone, he said, "Here, your mother and your wife would like to talk with you."

That was strange. Here I was, thirty-one years old, on the other side of the world, walking around in a remote cemetery, and a stranger comes up and hands me a cell phone with my mom and wife on the other line for a three-way call. (By the way, cell phones were not yet common.)

During that brief conversation I learned that my wife and mother were terrified about my whereabouts. I had forgotten to email them upon my arrival. And when they contacted the hotel, a clerical error showed that I had not yet arrived. I put them at ease, assuring them I was fine. I handed the phone back to the man, who explained he was from the U.S. embassy and had been sent specifically to find me. I thanked him.

But when the embassy official walked off, I realized that

kind of thing would never have happened in the early days of Christian missions. When those people boarded a ship in Liverpool or Halifax, there was no turning back. They brought with them a few boxes, and they were gone, usually for the rest of their lives. When they walked out onto those ships and waved goodbye to their friends and loved ones, they knew they were cutting ties. In many cases, that was the last glimpse they would ever catch of their homeland and their people.

Some might question whether their journey to the other side of the world to spread the gospel was even worth it. You had a good chance of dying at sea. If you made it to your destination you probably died within the first few years. You were certainly lonely, almost completely cut off from your own culture. There was no bank machine from which to draw money. You had to find a way to make a living unless you had managed to raise some support from back home. And support came perhaps once or twice a year in the form of a few letters and some cash to stock up on supplies. Of course, when the letters finally arrived they were already six months old.

Similar scenes played out all over the world: West Africa, South Africa, East Africa, South India, Burma, Southeast Asia, across the vast expanse of China, the Pacific Islands, Patagonia, the Caribbean. Missionaries boarded ships with a few boxes and made their long journey to the far reaches of the world, at a time when those places were virtually unknown.

And there I was, many years later, thinking about those

missionaries who were buried by their families in graves now dilapidated and nearly forgotten.

Why did they do it?

They did it because they believed in the gospel. And when they planted their Christian faith in all parts of the world, they probably never knew what would happen, or how magnificently it would grow.

This book is not a history of missions. Rather, it looks at the *results* of Christian missions. It is a book that describes the surprising rise of Christianity in the recent past. All over the world, the gospel was planted, sometimes five centuries ago, sometimes only a century ago. In the years since, however, something rather unpredictable occurred. Christianity blossomed. In Asia, Africa, Oceania, and Latin America, it grew prolifically. And while it grew, it took on characteristics of the cultures in which it was planted.

Ironically, while all of this activity was happening globally, Christianity in the Western world seemed to enter a period of decline. In Russia, the Soviets outlawed the church. In the Middle East, Christianity vanished almost entirely. In America, some polls proclaimed the great decline of the Christian faith. In Western Europe, it appeared Christianity had become a relic, something better suited for museums than for living, breathing human beings. Some wondered whether the era of Christianity was coming to an end.

But that's not happening. Not at all. Christianity is resurrecting. From its exponential growth in sub-Saharan Africa, to its revival in Russia, to the megachurch movements in

Asia, it is entering a period of unprecedented growth thanks to those lonely missionaries who gave all, sometimes just for a few converts. But those few converts in Africa, Asia, and Latin America carried the torch. They spread the gospel to their friends and their communities. All over their homelands, they sacrificed to spread the Christian gospel to others in their societies. Sometimes they too paid the ultimate price. And in those cases, their sons, daughters, friends, and sisters and brothers in Christ protected and carried the faith to other peoples and still other lands.

The story of Christianity's global rise continues to fascinate. Just when you thought Christianity was nearly dead in Britain, here come Caribbean and African immigrants, bringing the gospel back to the U.K. Just when it appeared as though Eastern Europe's dance with Christianity was over, it comes storming back alongside the Iron Curtain's fall. Just when American Christianity seemed to be ossifying, here come Latino and Asian immigrants, enlivening the faith in ways no one could have foreseen.

Christian missions today are from everywhere and to everywhere. Through immigrants, refugees, international travel, foreign students, and cross-cultural marriages, people from different backgrounds are mixing together like never before in history. And their faith is precious to them, so they carry it with them. Like the missionaries to Malaysia, many of these people put their faith first. Still today many are willing to sacrifice everything—even life itself—for Christ. But when they die, they become witnesses. And somehow, their trust in

God and passion for the faith catches on in the lives of those they leave behind.

Now I stand before students and lecture about new Christian movements in Africa, martyrs in Asia, pilgrimages in Europe, and revivals in Latin America. It is a fascinating story of what has happened in the wake of all of those isolated yet determined missionaries. I believe it is a story worth telling.

Christianity is rising. You just have to look around.

1

The Staggering Decline of Christianity in Western Europe

When I completed high school in 1991, my parents wanted to give me a graduation present. So they presented me with a choice: a computer or a trip to Europe. Easy decision. I packed my bags and was on my way in no time. It was my first time abroad and everything was so thrilling, especially the fact that the German flight crew allowed me to drink beer on the plane. I was traveling with my German friend—Oliver (pronounced Oh-lee-vah)—who had spent the year as an exchange student in my hometown of Portales, New Mexico, a small farming community known for its tasty peanuts.

I'm not proud of this, but my first day in Germany was a blur. Not only was this my first experience with jet lag, but when Oliver's mother went to work that first morning we went directly to the liquor cabinet. She was not impressed when she came home and found her son and his American friend completely inebriated. And this pattern continued for a few days. We went to the Hofbräuhaus in Munich, which was crowded with people drinking huge glasses of beer. When we got together with Oliver's friends, they all smoked and drank freely, without looking over their shoulders for somebody's parents. Oliver's parents were divorced; they too smoked and drank, and welcomed us to smoke and drink with them. They were all Catholic, but I didn't notice anybody going to church.

Where I grew up, in small-town New Mexico, divorce was taboo, we drank in secret, and we attended church three times a week—Sunday morning, Sunday night, and Wednesday night. For an eighteen-year-old who had scarcely seen life outside of my quiet, church-oriented village, my newfound freedom in Germany intoxicated me. The speed limit on the autobahn proved especially exhilarating . . . because there *was* no speed limit on the autobahn!

My first taste of Europe was all so unexpected. I had lived a sheltered life, never realizing how large an impact Christianity made in my little agricultural society until I left the United States for the first time. Almost everything in my town had something to do with church. We prayed before our sports events. We never held a practice of any sort on Sunday morning because everyone was in church (or was *supposed* to be). Every single one of us had a religious affiliation. And even though we sometimes drank beer, we usually felt guilty about it.

What astounded me, however, was the number of amazing churches in Germany. Churches on every block. And some of them were absolutely huge! They were by far the most amazing buildings that I had ever seen in my life. As Oliver and I drove east to Austria and Czechoslovakia, we encountered so many beautiful churches. And they were so holy and peaceful and impressive. But nobody was there. Just empty, cavernous temples. It made no sense to me. Europeans seemed so worldly, but there was also something quite religious about this place.

Changes in Western Europe

Society in Western Europe is changing dramatically. With an aging population and a very low fertility rate, European society is headed toward real challenges. On average, European women give birth to only one or two kids. This low fertility leads to a decline in the number of overall citizens. And this explains why the nations of Western Europe rely on immigrants. They need workers to sustain their economy. These workers are often not Christians. They bring their own religions and cultures to Europe. As a result, Europe is changing.[1]

Western Europeans are secular people today. They hardly

---

1. In my 2010 book *The Changing World of Christianity* (New York: Peter Lang) I used a typology consisting of eight cultural blocks: Western Europe, Eastern Europe, North America, Oceania, Asia, Latin America and the Caribbean, the Middle East, and Africa. I have adopted that same approach here.

attend church services. Religious norms are gone. The Christian fabric that characterized medieval "Christendom" is gone.

Christianity is connected deeply to European history. The Italians, French, Spanish, and Irish are virtually all Catholic, at least in name. For hundreds of years, Scandinavians were resolutely Lutheran. Some of Europe's nations—like Switzerland and Germany—are mixed, about half Protestant and half Catholic. But up to recent decades, they were all profoundly *Christian.*

But Western Europeans—in the birthplace of the Enlightenment—changed remarkably during the last half of the twentieth century. It is amazing to think that in 1900 the Europeans sailed all over the world, placing missionaries in some of the most remote places on earth. They had great success planting churches and cultivating new Christians virtually everywhere. By the end of the twentieth century, however, that religious excitement was long gone.

I remember a few years ago, my wife and I went to a church piano concert in Stockholm, Sweden. We arrived early, thinking the church might fill up. But when the concert began, only the two of us and another couple, along with the church caretaker, were there to enjoy the elegant music. It was weird, because outside the church building thousands of people walked around, eating and talking, completely disinterested. I felt sorry for the pianist. But she seemed to enjoy herself, even if her audience consisted only of five people.

Throughout my career, whether in conferences or while

conducting research, I have taken great interest in discussing religious matters with Europeans. Almost invariably they are happy to oblige. I have listened carefully to priests and pilgrims while visiting the Shroud of Turin in Italy, talked with travelers on trains, stayed up late with graduate students in Germany, and walked the cobblestone streets of Oxford and Cambridge with colleagues. In my conversations with these people from all walks of life, I discovered an interesting and rather surprising theme. They often explain that they have not completely abandoned the Christian faith. Rather, they have transformed it, and applied it toward new and different causes: human rights, climate issues, science and medicine, socialized healthcare, ambitious attempts to eradicate homelessness and poverty, acceptance of immigrants—including Muslim ones. They freely admit that they have abandoned the organized church. Sure, they might baptize, marry, and bury in the local parish, but that's about it. Most of my conversation partners see the collaboration of church and state as outdated. They welcome authentic and personal spirituality, however. Importantly, they don't despise the state church or the illustrious Christian past. They appreciate it. But they say those days are over. The state church idea has lost its relevance. New models for spirituality are needed to meet the growing need for alternative approaches to religion, faith, and belief in the supernatural.

Western Europeans learned valuable lessons from their horrifying experiences in the first half of the twentieth century. Americans must remember that the two world wars were mainly European wars, and they caused destruction on a scale unimaginable, in their own backyards. Americans can't really relate to this. We sent our boys "off" to fight. But Europeans rebuilt their buildings, cleared out the debris, and had to overcome their national hostilities toward each other. And they are reminded of their past with a vast network of tourist destinations such as concentration camps, military cemeteries, and pieces of the past that still stand—such as portions of the Berlin Wall.

But Western Europeans have now plunged their swords into ploughshares. They have become a peaceful society. They have turned away from their violent past and have embraced a much more tolerant way of thinking. Strangely, however, as Europeans turned their backs on catastrophic warfare with each other, they also turned away from their churches. For many Europeans, there was little difference between their religion and their politics. The two went hand in hand. And the reason they lost faith in their churches was because they lost faith in their politics. And there can be no doubt that Europe's churches were complicit in the world wars. Pastors and priests from state churches often blessed their combatants as they marched into battle.[2]

Europe understands the role of religion in broader society very differently than we do here in the United States. In Europe, the church and the state were almost always wedded together. To be a member of a European country meant

2. See Philip Jenkins, *The Great and Holy War: How World War I Became a Religious Crusade* (New York: HarperOne, 2014).

some of your tax money went to the church. It is still this way in many Western European nations, even in some of the most secular ones, such as in Scandinavia. The churches collect revenue from the state taxes. Church officials are considered employees of the state.

I once interviewed a German pastor who said her salary remains the same whether people come to services or not. And she receives a good salary with outstanding benefits. She is a state employee because she is an officially ordained pastor in an official Lutheran church. She lamented the fact that only three elderly women attend services regularly at her church, but she most certainly doesn't respect the American model where any Tom, Dick, or Harry can start their own church and teach anything they like. In her mind, religion is not something that should be linked to consumerism. The worship of God should be sanctioned at some level. Churches are not the same things as hamburger joints or coffee shops. It soils the sacredness of Christianity to use it as just another avenue for free enterprise.

The United States is so very different from Europe in this regard. For better or for worse, we *do* treat our churches like we treat our shops and businesses. They survive if they can sustain themselves, if they can attract attention and people and dollars.

In the United States we abandoned any hopes of cozy church-state relations very soon after the Constitution was written. In 1791 the First Amendment was adopted, specifying that "Congress shall make no law respecting an estab-

lishment of religion, or prohibiting the free exercise thereof."
Incidentally, that amendment was passed during the time
of the French Revolution (1789–1799), when the Catholic
Church was severed from the state in a violent series of events
that changed the course of French history. French society
changed suddenly, from being a Catholic society to practicing something the French call *laïcité*—"the absolute separation
of religion from politics."[3]

The French Revolution set into motion a long period of
tension between church and state in Western Europe. That
process increased rapidly in the post–World War II era, and
by 2010 the framers of the European Union's Constitution
made one thing clear: religion had lost the battle. In a
70,000-word document, the word "Christian" was nowhere
to be found. The French president remarked, "Europeans live
in a *purely secular* political system, where religion does not
play an important role."[4]

The lack of Christ or Christianity in the E.U. documents
was very telling. Christian Europe was finished. But there was
some irony, too. Emblazoned on the E.U. flag is the "Circle of Twelve Stars," which represents the Virgin Mary. Even
the artist who designed the flag openly admitted that it was
based on a passage from the book of Revelation: "And there
appeared a great sign in heaven; a woman clothed with the

3. Philip Jenkins, "The Legacy of Christendom," 136, in *The Wiley-Blackwell Companion to World Christianity*, ed. Lamin Sanneh and Michael McClymond (Oxford:
Wiley & Sons, 2016).
4. Jenkins, "The Legacy of Christendom," 137.

sun, and the moon under her feet, and upon her head a crown of twelve stars."[5]

The Old Guard

Scholars struggle to explain how Western Europe secularized so rapidly. In the early 1900s, the region was ablaze with Christian revivals, a massive and worldwide missionary enterprise, and an unbridled ambition to "evangelize the world in this generation." This was the well-known rally cry of Nobel Peace Prize winner John Mott. Imagine that. In 1946 the Nobel Peace Prize was awarded to a man who wanted to win the world to Jesus Christ. And his words resounded throughout the Western world. Europe took the lead in evangelizing the millions of non-Christians living in Asia and Africa and beyond.

By the early twenty-first century, however, former Pope Benedict XVI took an entirely different tone: "We are no longer able to hear God . . . God strikes us as pre-scientific, no longer suited for our age." The pope delivered this speech in his home country of Germany, where less than 15 percent of the population even bothers to attend church services anymore.[6]

Yes, even the Bishop of Rome—the head of the world's largest Christian denomination—had come to terms with the reality of the situation: God had vanished.

---

5. See Jenkins, "The Legacy of Christendom," 136. See Revelation 12:1.
6. Ian Fisher, "Pope Warns Against Secularization in Germany," *New York Times*, 10 September 2006, located at http://www.nytimes.com/2006/09/10/world/europe/11pope.web.html.

Conservative British politician Margaret Thatcher once weighed in on these issues. In a 1988 speech to the Church of Scotland—known as the "Sermon on the Mound"—Thatcher emphasized that Christianity was "a fundamental part of our national heritage. . . . We are a nation whose ideals are founded on the Bible." She envisioned a critical role for the church during changing times: "We Parliamentarians can legislate for the rule of law. . . . You, the church, can teach the life of faith." She ended her speech by reminding them that their service to the unseen kingdom of God is indelibly linked to their service on earth.[7]

But like Pope Benedict, Thatcher represents the old guard, which is fading fast. Their era is not over, but it is certainly fading.

We should be careful to point out that this old guard still has some influence. For example, several recent Prime Ministers are people of deep faith. Tony Blair is a very devoted Roman Catholic convert. Gordon Brown is a committed Presbyterian. Theresa May is the daughter of an Anglican priest, and she is often seen attending church services, even when there is no real political advantage for her to do so.[8] David Cameron came under intense fire for explicitly calling Britain a "Christian country" in some of his writings as well as in public speeches. But the fact that Cameron's comments

7. Margaret Thatcher, "Speech to General Assembly of the Church of Scotland," 21 May 1988, located at http://www.margaretthatcher.org/document/107246.
8. See Andrew Brown, "Theresa May Is a Religious Nationalist," *Foreign Policy*, 6 December 2016, located at http://foreignpolicy.com/2016/12/06/why-theresa-mays-english-doesnt-translate-to-america/.

were met with such criticism shows just how drastically the times have changed.[9]

Like the rest of Western Europe, the U.K. is now largely secular. In 2016, half of the English population claimed to have "no religion" at all.[10] In the popular media as well as in academic writing, these people are often referred to as the "religious nones." When asked for their religious preference, they simply reply, "None."

Even Britain's funerals are now mainly secular. Of the top ten funeral songs in Britain, only three are religious. The top funeral song in the U.K. is Frank Sinatra's "My Way." The top religious song played at funerals is "The Lord Is My Shepherd," but it has fallen to fifth place.[11] These statistics should not be too surprising, however, for a nation where more people believe in extraterrestrials than believe in God.[12]

All across Europe, parish churches are closing, people are looking elsewhere for spiritual answers, and the big state churches face a new reality: they no longer have much social influence. For example, the German Catholic establishment—which is disintegrating—provides some insight here.

9. Michael McGough, "Britain a 'Christian country'? Careful there, prime minister!," *Los Angeles Times*, 23 April 2014, located at http://www.latimes.com/opinion/opinion-la/la-ol-cameron-britain-christianity-20140423-story.html.

10. Stephen Bullivant, *Contemporary Catholicism in England and Wales: A statistical report based on recent British Social Attitudes survey data* (London: St. Mary's University Twickenham, 2016), located at https://www.stmarys.ac.uk/research/centres/benedict-xvi/contemporary-catholicism.aspx.

11. These statistics come from the website "British Religion in Numbers," located at http://www.brin.ac.uk/2016/counting-religion-in-britain-september-2016/.

12. Andrew Higgins, "A More Secular Europe, Divided by the Cross," *New York Times*, 17 June 2013, located at http://www.nytimes.com/2013/06/18/world/europe/a-more-secular-europe-divided-by-the-cross.html.

In 2014 and 2015 combined, around 400,000 German adults left the Catholic Church. That's in comparison with only around 9000 adults who join each year. Baptism rates are in steep decline. Since that unforgettable and glorious moment of reunification at the Berlin Wall in 1990, the Catholic Church's membership has nosedived from 43 percent of Germany's total population to 24 percent in 2015.[13]

When Americans travel to Western Europe, we stand in awe of the ornate basilicas, splendid monasteries, and breathtaking cathedrals. We imagine a vibrant Christian world where monks chanted, church bells rang, choirs sang, and an air of holiness penetrated the society. But if we look beneath the surface, we quickly realize that Christianity is part of Europe's history, not its present. Europe's churches—those cavernous monuments of a Christian past—are filled only with tourists like ourselves, gazing upon relics and memories rather than present realities.

Christianity collapsed in Europe because of widespread resentment against the church for its collaboration with demented political leaders during the world wars. It collapsed because of corruption in the churches themselves. It collapsed because Christian leaders—supposedly pious men who were deeply trusted—succumbed to such horrors as pedophilia, inside their *churches*, with hideous cover-ups. The blame must not be placed on the people. They simply voted with their feet. They gave up on their churches. The liabilities began

---

13. "The Catholic Church in Germany," *Deutsche Bischofskonferenz*, located at http://www.dbk.de/en/katholische-kirche/katholische-kirche-deutschland/.

to outweigh the blessings of the church. The church abandoned its prophetic voice for political clout. The churches lost touch with the people. They received their money whether they worked for it or not.

Christianity collapsed in Europe because of people like "the Bishop of Bling." His real name is Franz–Peter Tebartz–van Elst. When Pope Francis came to power he fired this German bishop for spending $43 million from the church treasury just to renovate his home. The Bishop of Bling is but one more well-justified reason for why Europeans are suspicious of the church. The official state churches have made such patently stupid mistakes. In the past they were able to get away with some of this, but in an internet age where information is so easily accessible, the state churches have had to use more discretion. In the case of the Bishop of Bling, he underestimated the power of information. He also underestimated Pope Francis's commitment to reform.[14]

The case of the Bishop of Bling illustrates how out of touch the European state-churches have become. For centuries they enjoyed profound privilege from the government, from the citizenry, and from their own church hierarchies. But times are changing. Thanks to the internet and more open access to information, these kinds of shenanigans trigger whistleblowers. Clergymen don't need $43-million renovations to their medieval castles. Church members don't want

---

14. Terrence McCoy, "How the 'Bishop of Bling' spent million renovating this house," *The Washington Post*, 28 March 2004, located at https://www.washingtonpost.com/news/morning-mix/wp/2014/03/28/how-the-bishop-of-bling-spent-43-million-renovating-this-house/?utm_term=.cfed4e587875.

to support these kinds of things anymore. In the medieval world it was normal. But today, people would rather their money help the homeless, support orphanages, or contribute to famine relief.

European churches are in trouble. Wherever we place the blame, one thing is clear: the Christian faith is spiraling downward in Europe. Thousands of church buildings have been converted to offices, gyms, pubs, warehouses, carpet stores, skateboard parks, apartments, libraries, homes, tire shops, concert halls, and even mosques. Some of the stories are downright bizarre. For example, St. Paul's church in Bristol, England, was turned into a circus training school.[15]

This process is playing out all across Europe, and on a massive scale. Two-thirds of the Roman Catholic churches in the Netherlands are set to close down by 2025. Nearly two hundred Protestant churches close per year in the Netherlands as well. The Church of England closes about twenty churches per year. In Germany, the Roman Catholic Church shutters churches at a rate of around fifty per year.

Christian Europe no longer exists. According to Pew Research, of the world's top-ten Christian nations (nations with the most Christians), only one is found in Europe: Germany. But it is very hard to call Germany a Christian nation anymore, since only 15 percent of them *ever* attend church.

---

15. Naftali Bendavid, "Europe's Empty Churches Go on Sale," *The Wall Street Journal*, 2 January 2015, located at https://www.wsj.com/articles/europes-empty-churches-go-on-sale-1420245359. See also Jesse Coburn, "As German Church Becomes Mosque, Neighbors Start to Shed Unease," *New York Times*, 23 July 2015, located at https://www.nytimes.com/2015/07/24/world/europe/as-german-church-becomes-mosque-neighbors-start-to-shed-unease.html?_r=0.

The future of Christianity belongs to other nations on that top-ten list: Mexico, Brazil, China, Philippines, Nigeria, Ethiopia, and the D. R. Congo.[16]

Signs of Hope

There are occasional signs that Christianity might have some life left in it, but not because of Western Europeans themselves. Rather, immigrants are providing European Christianity with hope for the future. Caribs, Poles, and Africans are setting up church in storefronts, homes, and in the back rooms of gigantic basilicas. I once attended a vibrant Protestant church service hidden at the rear of a massive Catholic church building in Turin, Italy. In order to access the gathering, you have to actually leave the Catholic sanctuary and walk outside and around to a separate entrance at the back of the church. It was not easy to find, but the little Protestant gathering of around fifty worshipers was refreshing and truly uplifting for me. There were no Italians in the group; however, this friendly and enthusiastic family of believers was like a mosaic from all over the world. Interestingly, this Protestant gathering outnumbered the attendees of the regular Catholic service in the main building. It made me wonder if immigration might actually turn Italy into a Protestant nation over time.

There are a few signs for hope in the United Kingdom, too. A recent study of thirteen churches in East London

16. See Pew Research Center's "Global Christianity" report, 19 December 2011, located at http://www.pewforum.org/2011/12/19/global-christianity-exec/.

discovered that some of them are in fact growing. Nine of the churches studied are majority Black congregations, and several have a significant Asian presence. Only two of them are relatively large: the Pentecostal one and the Catholic one, both with memberships in excess of eight hundred. They are both non-white churches, and are thriving in every way. Indeed the big picture here is that Britain's growing churches are typically non-white.[17]

These growing churches tend to be conservative, too. Trends in the British churches support a rather widespread thesis developed over the last few decades that while theologically progressive churches tend to shrink, conservative ones often thrive. In the British study cited above, the success of the Pentecostal and Catholic churches supports that thesis. One of the most striking theories coming from sociologists is that conservative congregations grow even when holding membership in a liberal or mainline denomination.[18]

17. See Beth Green, Angus Ritchie, and Tim Thorlby, *Church Growth in East London: A Grassroots View* (London: Center for Theology and Community, 2016), located at http://www.theology-centre.org.uk/wp-content/uploads/2013/04/Church-Grow th-digital.pdf. A summary of the findings is at http://www.brin.ac.uk/2016/count-ing-religion-in-britain-september-2016/.
18. David Haskell, Kevin Flatt, and Stephanie Burgoyne, "Theology Matters: Compar-ing the Traits of Growing and Declining Mainline Protestant Church Attendees and Clergy," *Review of Religious Research* 58, no. 4 (December 2016), located at http://link.springer.com/article/10.1007/s13644-016-0255-4. Haskell cites many studies with similar conclusions by Kelley, Iannaccone, Stark, Finke, Bibby, Burkin-shaw, Bowen, Flatt, and more. A summary of the findings was published by Haskell, "Liberal churches are dying. But conservative churches are thriving," *The Washington Post*, 4 January 2017, located at https://www.washingtonpost.com/posteverything/ wp/2017/01/04/liberal-churches-are-dying-but-conservative-churches-are-thriv-ing/?utm_term=.b1a74fff98b0. See also Rodney Stark and Roger Finke, *Acts of Faith: Explaining the Human Side of Religion* (Oakland: University of California Press, 2000).

Not only are they more conservative, but immigrants to the Western world from the global south tend to practice their religion much more than White Westerners do. Thus with more immigration to the West comes more active participation in church life. Think of all of those midweek Bible studies that we Americans attended in yesteryear. Those frequent gatherings still go on in global south churches. I remember one time in India I tried to keep pace with an Indian pastor as he distributed charity to church members, mediated family arguments, performed baptisms and healings, and traveled vast distances by jeep on poor roads to evangelize. I absolutely ran myself ragged trying to keep up with him, and I became sick. My hosts routinely stayed up late worshiping, held devotionals before bed, and prayed fervently at the breakfast table. The lesson I learned was that you have to be in excellent physical shape to be a pastor in India!

And similar to the culture of my youth in New Mexico, global southerners still place a very high value on church membership. Everybody who is somebody is a member of a congregation. That's where you get plugged in to your culture.

Another reason for church growth among global south Christians is simple: fertility. They have more kids than White Europeans. And when immigrants arrive in Britain, or in Western Europe in general, they tend to join faith communities with people like themselves—other likeminded immigrants from socially and theologically conservative places. They also marry at a younger age than Westerners, start their families earlier, and have more kids. Thus their families and churches grow larger, and faster. And their kids go to church. As a result, majority White churches often become majority non-white in a short period of time.

Immigration might be the saving grace for Western European churches. The Church of England has been devastated by membership losses. In 1983, England was nearly half Anglican. By 2014 that number had fallen to 19 percent. And without immigrants, the churches would be even emptier than they are now. The immigrants are providing Western European churches with a little hope.[19]

The churches of Scotland, for example, are in terrible shape. Scotland's "religious none" (no religious affiliation) population is now over 50 percent. Church of Scotland membership has collapsed. It is likely that within a few decades Scotland will have more Catholics than members of the Church of Scotland. But even still, church is out. Secularization is in. Scottish society has abandoned Christianity faster than almost any other on record. And what is perhaps most telling is that among those in Scotland who declare themselves as being "religious," a full two-thirds of them say they either *never or practically never* attend services! You know

---

19. See Bullivant, cited above. After adjusting for inflation, overall income in the Church of England "has dropped by 5% since 2004 and planned giving by 8% since 2009, while expenditure has remained fairly steady." See "Parish Finance Statistics 2014," provided by The Church of England Research and Statistics, located at https://www.churchofengland.org/media/2853794/2014financestatistics.pdf. See also Clive Field, "Church of England parochial finance," 1 October 2016, located at http://www.brin.ac.uk/2016/counting-religion-in-britain-september-2016/.

Christianity is in trouble in Scotland if even the *most* religious don't even bother to go to church.[20]

A few years ago I was in Dundee, Scotland, doing some research at the university. On Sunday I went out looking for a church to attend and decided to go to The Gate, a nondenominational church in the city led by a husband-and-wife team. It was a marvelous service, and I left feeling uplifted and encouraged. It is a multiracial congregation and has a whole host of ministries in the city. The service was lively and the pastors—Gordon and Fiona Stewart—were engaging and innovative. They connected with the audience in a way that most Church of Scotland congregations simply don't. They greeted me after services and even invited me to their home for lunch, which I eagerly accepted. While I don't have much hope for Scotland's national denomination, I do believe that there are churches like The Gate scattered across Europe that might offer a more optimistic future.

The Spanish Model

All things considered, the Roman Catholic Church fares slightly better than the Protestant churches of Western Europe. But even in strongly Catholic countries—such as Ireland, France, Spain, Portugal, Italy, and Austria—the church struggles to retain its former relevance in society. Were it not

20. See "Most people in Scotland 'not religious'," *BBC News*, 3 April 2016, located at http://www.bbc.com/news/uk-scotland-35953639. See the 2011 Scottish census results on religion at http://www.gov.scot/Topics/People/Equality/Equalities/Data-Grid/Religion/RelPopMig.

for taxes, subsidies, and government funding, many of these churches would be forced to close their doors.

Fortunately, however, the failure of Christianity in Europe is not the whole story. For instance, Spain is beginning to see something of a Christian renaissance. It seems the church may have hit bottom in the aftermath of the devastating economic crisis of 2008—which Spain has still not recovered from. Church attendance bottomed out at around 12 percent nationally. By 2012, however, that number was on the rise.[21]

Ironically, since the economic collapse, more Spaniards are giving to the church. Seminarians are increasing as well. Youth are joining monasteries and convents in greater numbers than we've seen in years. The Poor Clares community is growing, and in 2010 the Vatican approved the founding of a new sub-order of the Poor Clares called *Iesu Communio*, otherwise known as the "sisters in jeans" because of their denim habits. They are comprised mainly of younger women. (I keep my eye on the Poor Clares since I named my eldest daughter "Clare" after the famous nun who worked alongside St. Francis of Assisi.)

A famous Spanish model and actress named Olalla Oliveros recently made headlines when she quit her career in order to join a convent. The Catholic news reported, "A face at one time seen on countless billboards across Spain is now adorned with blue sackcloth and veil." At the age of thirty-six, Olalla's decision was greeted with shock, but there was a

21. For Spain's recent religious revival, see Filip Mazurczak, "Is Spain Regaining Its Faith?," *First Things*, 11 June 2014, located at https://www.firstthings.com/web-exclusives/2014/06/is-spain-regaining-its-faith.

certain sense of admiration in the media toward her for making that move.[22]

Olalla was at the height of her career when she made the decision. But it was not a sudden decision. She gave it much thought and postponed joining the cloistered Order of Saint Michael after weighing the implications for her life. Complicating her decision was the fact that she had just been offered the lead role in a blockbuster film.

Olalla's decision came after she visited the famous Fatima Chapel in Portugal and had an "earthquake" experience. Roman Catholics revere this place as the location where Mary, the Mother of God, revealed herself to three shepherd children in 1917, during the thick of World War I. The apparitions caused a huge stir in the Catholic Church due to prophecies and "The Three Secrets" supposedly revealed to the children by the Virgin Mary. The site is now a basilica in the Catholic Church, and visitors often claim to have intensely spiritual experiences while there.

Olalla's earthquake moment came when she had inexplicable visions of herself wearing a nun's habit, and could not rid herself of the images in her mind. She concluded that God was speaking to her, encouraging her to follow him into the cloister. She publicly commented, "The Lord is never wrong. He asked if I will follow him, and I could not refuse." Olalla claimed she had grown tired of being a model for sexual

---

22. "Spanish model quits glamorous career to become a nun," *Catholic Online*, 23 June 2014, located at http://www.catholic.org/news/hf/faith/story.php?id=55906. The incident was reported widely in the Spanish media and in Catholic media.

immorality and commercial purposes, and instead chose to be a model that "promotes the true dignity of women."

Merkel's Germany

"We don't have too much Islam, we have too little Christianity."

Those were the words of Angela Merkel when she was speaking to her political party—the Christian Democratic Union—in 2010 while serving as Chancellor of Germany. Merkel was addressing the issue of Muslim immigration. Rather than advocating the building of walls or increased restrictions on immigration numbers, she was actually trying to get her party to see that they are a Christian party, with Christian convictions, and should therefore open their doors to immigrants. Applause broke out when she added, "We have too few discussions about the Christian view of mankind . . . about the values that guide us and about our Judeo-Christian tradition."[23]

Hold on a second. Germany is now a secular country. Christianity has plummeted there. And yet, the *Chancellor of Germany* urged her *Christian* political party to take a stand for their faith in a nation where hardly anybody practices their faith anymore. Germans may not practice Christianity these days, but they have inherited so much of the faith that it would be impossible for them to completely sever ties.

23. See Tom Heneghan, "Merkel urges Germans: stand up for Christian values," *Reuters*, 16 November 2010, located at http://in.reuters.com/article/us-germany-cdu-christianity-idINTRE6AE3K520101115. The full speech is located at http://www.karlsruhe2010.cdu.de/images/stories/docs/101115-Rede-Merkel.pdf.

Merkel won the debate within her party, but not without a fight. Some opposed her, saying Muslims were often less educated, more likely to get on welfare, and less likely to contribute to the national economy. Many feared Germany might accidentally allow terrorists to come inside the nation if they were to take an open-door policy. But Merkel persisted. She tried to get people to see that not only was her party a *Christian* party but the German nation was built on Christian foundations. She urged them to extend hospitality to immigrants, and to respect the nation's principles of religious freedom. Jesus commanded his followers to welcome strangers, love enemies, and care for others regardless of their religious or ethnic background. That's the point of the Parable of the Good Samaritan.

Let's now fast-forward to 2014 when Germany accepted 577,000 immigrants. Then in 2015 they accepted nearly two million more due largely to chaos in the Middle East, especially in Syria. Critics argued that Chancellor Merkel's open-door policy would backfire. Merkel, however, seemed more committed to her Christian beliefs on these matters than to political winds.[24]

Angela Merkel was born in 1954 in communist East Germany. Her father served as a Lutheran pastor in a context where faith was repressed. There is little doubt that some of

---

24. See Lewis Sanders, "Two million: Germany records largest influx of immigrants in 2015," *DW (Deutsche Welle)*, 12 March 2016, located at http://www.dw.com/en/two-million-germany-records-largest-influx-of-immigrants-in-2015/a-19131436. Also see Damon Linker, "How Angela Merkel imperiled Europe's future," *The Week*, 5 August 2016.

her father's resilience rubbed off on her. She has described her faith in God as being her "constant companion."[25]

By looking at how Merkel's Christian convictions shape her politics, we might be led to believe that Germany is a strongly Christian society. But in reality Christianity's numbers are in sharp decline in Germany, and have been for decades. Almost all of those big, beautiful churches are relics. They are monuments to what used to be, not to what is happening today.

Nevertheless, the fact that Merkel—a committed Christian—has such clout in Germany seems to hint at Christianity's continued relevance. When the leader of Europe's most powerful nation repeatedly invokes Christian values, we must take notice. Christianity may look dead in Europe. But when Europe's most important leaders emphasize their Christian heritage, we have to wonder whether those reports of Christianity's death—even in Western Europe—have been greatly exaggerated.

The Future of Faith in Western Europe

In recent years there has been a large-scale debate over Islam's presence in Western Europe. And certainly Christianity's future is tied to Islam's future in the region. Without doubt, Islam is growing there. Many Muslims from conflicted areas of the world are desperate to emigrate to the West, and up

---

25. Erasmus, "German politicians are both more and less religious than British ones," *The Economist*, 7 January 2016, located at http://www.economist.com/blogs/erasmus/2016/01/germany-britain-and-religion.

until recent years Western Europe was very accommodating to them. And while some Europeans are now showing misgivings, tolerance is still far more common. For example, in 2016 the residents of London elected Sadiq Khan, a practicing Muslim, as the city's mayor. In the city of Rotterdam, in the Netherlands, Ahmed Aboutaleb—the son of a Moroccan Muslim cleric—has served as mayor since 2009. There are other examples like these.

As of now, about 7 percent of Western Europe's population is Muslim, and that figure is rising due to several factors. First is the issue of immigration. Several Muslim societies have collapsed into anarchy or worse. Sectarian violence, economic stagnation, political chaos, and a massive scarcity of jobs have caused millions of Muslims to try to get out of their home countries. There is no way to know whether these people will become secular or will hold onto their faith over the long term. The power of secularization in Europe is strong, with few signs of easing up.[26]

Second, Muslims in Europe are, on average, younger than their Western European counterparts by nearly a decade. The average European Muslim is aged thirty-two—right in the midst of the most productive childbearing years.[27]

Third, Muslims have higher fertility rates than typical Western Europeans, which will boost their numbers in coming years. And the Western world relies on immigration to

---

26. Conrad Hackett, "5 Facts about the Muslim population in Europe," *Pew Research Center*, 19 July 2016, located at http://www.pewresearch.org/fact-tank/2016/07/19/5-facts-about-the-muslim-population-in-europe/.
27. See Hackett, "5 Facts about the Muslim population in Europe."

keep its economies moving. Without enough workers and consumers, economies go into recession.[28] The bottom line is that whether Europeans *want* immigrants may not really matter. They *need* them.

It is too early to say this is the end of Christianity in Europe. Indeed, other forms of spirituality are filling the void, such as New Age beliefs, the rise of Islam, and attempts to return to the pre-Christian religions of Europe. For example, a few years ago, my wife and I were surprised to meet some Scandinavian doctoral students who firmly believe in elves.

Scholars have shown that despite the decline of formal Christianity in Europe, spirituality and belief in supernatural beings persists. One sociologist, Abby Day, claims that during her many interviews with British citizens, she found widespread belief in ghosts. She also discovered that many of her interviewees believed their deceased ancestors were present, and they could even contact them.[29] Yes, these are the supposedly nonreligious people. Her point was that while Europeans commonly refer to themselves as being irreligious, when you do a little digging beneath the surface—for exam-

---

28. Islam has a long tradition of forbidding contraception, and thus Muslim families tend to be comparatively large. While this teaching is not universal within Islam, conservative leaders tend to cite the Qur'an (17:31 and 6:151), which states: "Do not kill your children for fear of poverty. We provide for them and for you. Indeed their killing is ever a great sin." Sahih International Version. Alternatively, Western Europe's fertility rate has plummeted to around 1.56 children per woman; Eastern Europe's is the lowest in the world: 1.38. In the Middle East it is around 2.88; in Africa 4.72; in Asia 2.35; in North America 2.05. See Dyron Daughrity, *The Changing World of Christianity* (New York: Peter Lang, 2010).

29. Abby Day, *Believing in Belonging: Belief and Social Identity in the Modern World* (Oxford: Oxford University Press, 2011).

ple in qualitative interviews—you'll find some very striking religious beliefs.

But for the present time, it is most certainly the case that organized Christianity is in trouble in Western Europe. Consider the following vignettes:

- Only 50 percent of Italians consider themselves to be Catholic, and 20 percent of Italians claim to be atheists. Italy is supposed to be home to the Roman Catholic Church, not a place that is but half Catholic.[30]

- In what was widely viewed as a sign of things to come, a primary school in Spain was ordered to remove all crucifixes from its walls after a four-year court battle.[31]

- In the Netherlands, one in six *of the clergy* is either agnostic or atheist.[32] Imagine that—an atheist pastor. How odd it must be to confide in your pastor that you're having doubts, only to learn he's a nonbeliever.

- Brussels, the de facto capital of the European Union, has twice as many practicing Muslims as practicing Christians.[33]

30. Josephina McKenna, "Poll: Only 50 percent of Italians call themselves Catholic," *Religion News Service*, 29 March 2016, located at http://religionnews.com/2016/03/29/poll-only-50-percent-of-italians-call-themselves-catholic/.

31. Rachel Donadio, "Spain Is a Battleground for Church's Future," *New York Times*, 5 January 2009, located at http://www.nytimes.com/2009/01/06/world/europe/06church.html.

32. Robert Pigott, "Dutch rethink Christianity for a doubtful world," *BBC News*, 5 August 2011, located at http://www.bbc.com/news/world-europe-14417362.

33. Erasmus, "In and around Brussels, the practice of Islam is outstripping Christianity," *The Economist*, 18 February 2016, located at http://www.economist.com/blogs/erasmus/2016/02/belgium-christianity-and-islam.

- In Ireland, church attendance has dropped from over 90 percent in the 1970s to less than 14 percent today.[34]
- Luxembourg, for centuries a Catholic nation, recently jettisoned religious instruction in schools. Priests will no longer receive their pay from public funds, and all church property will be placed into a charitable trust. The Catholic seminary will be converted into an "interfaith learning center."[35]

In Western Europe today, the burden of proof is not so much on atheists and agnostics to explain why they walked away from faith. Rather, the burden of proof is on people of faith to explain why they persist in their religion. Religion is now somewhat exotic, peculiar, and worth questioning. Today in Western Europe, the irreligious people have become the normal ones.

I realize that for Christians this chapter is probably a bit depressing. The staggering decline of Christianity in Western Europe is difficult to comprehend for those of us who place our hope in Christ and believe firmly in the institution of the church. Christians should not lose heart, however, because—globally—there is an entirely different story being told. In fact, the future of Christianity shines bright and pow-

---

34. Douglas Dalby, "Catholic Church's Hold on Schools at Issue in Changing Ireland," *New York Times*, 21 January 2016, located at https://www.nytimes.com/2016/01/22/world/europe/ireland-catholic-baptism-school.html?_r=0.

35. Frank Cranmer and David Pocklington, "Luxembourg moves towards further separation of religion and the state," *Law and Religion UK*, 28 January 2015, located at http://www.lawandreligionuk.com/2015/01/28/luxembourg-moves-towards-further-separation-of-religion-and-the-state/.

erful when we look outside the Western world. Yes, it is magnificent what is happening.

Over in Russia, for example, it is a completely different story than the one we just read. In fact it is pretty much the opposite. To that part of the world we now turn.

2

The Death and Resurrection of Christianity in Russia

As a young man raised in rural New Mexico, the 1984 movie *Red Dawn* inspired me. Filmed in my home state, it featured two of Hollywood's biggest stars: Patrick Swayze and Charlie Sheen. The premise of the film captivated my generation's imagination. Sitting in class one day, some small-town high school kids look out the window and notice Russians parachuting down, landing near the school. The teacher is immediately killed and some of the students escape and hide, while the rest of the town is dealt with mercilessly. Fortunately, one of the teenagers leads his buddies to his dad's well-stocked gun shop where they load up on artillery and mount a powerful resistance. By the end of the film, however, the "Wolverines"—as the teenagers called themselves—are dead, but their courage lives on and they are commemorated by the United

States for their great valor in protecting the homeland. Oh yeah, I wanted to be those guys!

In the news media, Russians were always portrayed poorly. We believed they cheated in all the Olympics, and that's the only reason they were competitive. We believed they were atheists who controlled massive stockpiles of nuclear missiles, and were fully capable of launching them.

If *Red Dawn* wasn't enough, the following year we all watched *Rocky IV*—the most successful of the Rocky movies—where the huge Russian boxer stood like Goliath over Rocky (the American David) and warned him sternly at the outset of their fight: "I must break you." You know the iconic scene: James Brown dances around singing "Living in America" as Vegas showgirls dance excitedly in the background, holding American flags. Rocky eventually outlasts the giant in a bloody, hard-hitting, vicious duel. The victorious American wraps himself in the Stars and Stripes and all of us walked out of the theater feeling like we had really stuck it to those Russians!

The truth of the matter is that we were being indoctrinated. At a very basic level, all of that propaganda represented our attempts to overcome our paralyzing fear. We were afraid of Russia because we didn't understand them.

Aside from 11 September 2001, the most gripping live television scene I have ever witnessed was 9 November 1989, when the Berlin Wall began to be smashed by common Germans with their hammers as they declared freedom after decades of Soviet dominance. Those scenes were so powerful and so unforeseen. Only two years prior, in 1987, President Reagan proved to be prophetic when he publicly declared, right there in front of Berlin's Brandenburg Gate, "Mr. Gorbachev, open this gate. Mr. Gorbachev, tear down this wall." The crowds went wild, and we all teared up, so proud of our own freedom, and so sad that East Germany had to exist under the iron fist of the evil empire itself.

The truth, however, was that we were shocked when, seemingly out of nowhere, that wall did get torn down—on worldwide television. In just a matter of days, the powerful Soviet Union was finished. We Americans were now the unrivaled superpower in the world! We had overcome the enemy! We had prevailed!

Immediately, many Christian groups, including Roman Catholics, sent missionaries into Russia to evangelize. Yes, even our enemies needed the gospel. We delivered them Bibles, and we proceeded to establish churches all over that massive nation. We were going to save the Russians. Just a few years earlier Americans were in the midst of a long "Cold War" with Russia. Suddenly we were baptizing our former enemies into Christ.

Russia had become a mission territory, and we believed God wanted us to reach out to them. After all, they weren't so bad. Once we got past the whole Communism thing, we were able to see that they were humans too, in need of God's grace. Even our young, charismatic president, Bill Clinton, and his hard-drinking Russian counterpart, Boris Yeltsin, hugged each other and laughed like long-lost friends on the evening news. Arms around each other, the presidential bromance showed the world that Cold War prejudices were thawing. Russians could become friends to us, even buddies, perhaps even brothers and sisters in Christ. A new era had dawned.

Putin's Unexpected Impact

But then in the year 2000 Vladimir Putin entered the scene. Americans were immediately suspicious of Yeltsin's successor, primarily because it was quickly found out that he was a former KGB intelligence officer. Yeltsin was affable and open, the kind of guy you could stay up late cracking jokes with. But he was a terrible president. Corruption soared, the economy tanked, and it was very clear Yeltsin was not only widely unpopular in his home country, he was incompetent.

Putin was a very different animal. He was perceived as being stern, secretive (remember, he was KGB), and defensive. On his watch, Russia started to regain some of its lost glory. Its economy began to rebound after Yeltsin's disastrously sudden shift from socialism to free-market capitalism—leading to the oligarchy situation that remains. Yeltsin's policies allowed a few already-wealthy entrepreneurs to gorge themselves by eating up most major industries.

Under Putin's leadership, however, Russia's confidence began coming back around. And, quietly, after decades of forced silence, the Russian Orthodox Church emerged from the shadows. The church's patriarch began appearing at public events. Bishops were called upon by the government to participate in state ceremonies. Travelers noticed churches under construction.

Further, it was revealed that Putin himself claims to be a Christian, and was counting on the church to help him forge a common Russian identity after years of confusion and malaise. By joining forces with the Russian Orthodox Church, he thought he could help to redevelop Russian society and rehabilitate its reputation on the global stage. He took the church's lead in its promotion of conservative values, such as various anti-LGBT measures as well as pro-life causes. Some pro-democracy groups interpreted Putin's approach as being decidedly draconian: "Fall in line with the emphasis on family and religious values, or lose funding, or worse."[1] But the bigger picture was that Christianity's fortunes in Russia had changed dramatically.

In August of 2000 Putin visited an important monastery and spent an hour in private conversation with a revered monk, and afterwards wrote the following in the monastery's guestbook: "The revival of Russia and the growth of its might are unthinkable without the strengthening of society's moral foundations. The role and significance of the Russian Orthodox Church are huge. May God protect you."[2]

We Americans are skeptical when it comes to Russia, and for good reasons. The atrocities that occurred there in the

---

1. Rachel Donadio, "Russian Artists Face a Choice: Censor Themselves, or Else," *New York Times*, 1 April 2015, located at https://www.nytimes.com/2015/04/02/arts/international/russian-artists-face-a-choice-censor-themselves-or-else.html?_r=0.
2. Sophia Kishkovsky, "Russians See Church and State Come Closer," *New York Times*, 31 October 2012, located at http://www.nytimes.com/2012/11/01/world/europe/russians-see-orthodox-church-and-state-come-closer.html.

twentieth century are not easily forgotten: the gulag, wars, clandestine killings, constant surveillance of its people, curtailing of human rights, one of the worst persecutions of Christians on record, and more. Whether or not Putin is a tyrant, a pious believer, a power-drunk oligarch, or the reason for Russia's comeback, one thing is certain: Christianity in Russia has resurrected.

Putin represents a complete about-face when it comes to Russia's relationship with the church. After decades of brutal suppression of the faith, he has completely changed his nation's course when it comes to state relations with the Russian Orthodox Church. American Christians tend to frown upon the politicization of the church. We believe the church thrives when it is free from state control.

Orthodox Christians, however, have a long history of *symphonia*—where church and state complement and validate one another. The Russian Orthodox Church and Vladimir Putin are forging a new symphonic identity that brings church and state close together. Indeed Patriarch Kirill—the head of the Russian Orthodox Church—has praised Putin's rule over the nation as "a miracle from God."[3] Not only has Putin *allowed* the Orthodox Church to try and re-Christianize Russian society, he has been its greatest cheerleader (although a manly man who hunts tigers would likely disapprove of my word choice here).

Putin received acclaim in his country for bringing the

---

3. Rob Garver, "Putin's Calculated Revival of the Russian Orthodox Church," *The Fiscal Times*, 9 June 2015, located at http://www.thefiscaltimes.com/2015/06/09/Putins-Calculated-Revival-Russian-Orthodox-Church.

Winter Olympics to Russia in 2014. For those of us who watched the Russian economy collapse less than three decades ago, and heard horror stories of how Russia had become a mere shadow of itself, this was hard to fathom. A clear signal had been sent: Russia was back. And it was Putin who was widely perceived by Russians as being *the* point person who caused all of this to happen. Some think Russia has gained even too much confidence, evidenced in its return to being a major player in world events and the rapid rise of its military. But political developments aside, Russia's spiritual landscape is more vibrant than it has been in a hundred years.

How Christianity Nearly Died in Russia

Russians can tell you exactly when their nation officially embraced Jesus Christ. It was in the year 988 when their king—Vladimir the Great—converted to Christianity and required the same of his subjects, becoming a Christian kingdom virtually overnight. It is a good story.

It all begins with the conversion of the Slavic people by two Greek brothers held in the highest esteem today in the Slavic churches: Cyril and Methodius. They are known as the apostles to the Slavs due to their impressive missionary work in the ninth century. Not only did they evangelize vast regions—Moravia, Bulgaria, Serbia, Ukraine—but they also created an alphabet that is still used in the churches: Old Church Slavonic. Their goal was nothing less than to Christianize the people by teaching them to read the Bible and to worship in a common tongue. In these endeavors they succeeded brilliantly. Much of Eastern Europe is Christian today and nobody was more responsible for this development than the two Greek brothers from Thessaloniki.

Missionaries sent by the Byzantine (Eastern Orthodox) church spread the gospel all around central and eastern Europe for decades after the famed brothers. But something fortuitous happened in the tenth century that would seal the deal. In the 950s, a Russian princess named Olga of Kiev converted to Christ and propagated the Christian faith with enthusiasm. Olga's grandson was King Vladimir, the one who is credited with Christianizing Russia. (Never underestimate the influence of a grandmother!)

Olga's precocious grandson, King Vladimir, married a Byzantine queen named Anna and formally connected the courts of Russia to Byzantium (or, Constantinople)—at the time the most important city in Christendom.

Historians like to point out that in the history of Christianity, there have been three Romes—meaning major political centers for the faith. The first Rome was, of course, in Italy. However, when Rome was overrun by barbarians, Constantinople (modern-day Istanbul) emerged as the New Rome. But as various Islamic empires overran Constantinople, the new center of Christianity moved north to Russia. That's why today Moscow is called the Third Rome. And in many ways, especially architecturally, it lives up to its reputation.

Russian Christianity spread widely over the centuries, primarily due to the monastic movement. All across the lands we now call Russia, Orthodox monks established monasteries that actually served as conduits for endless little towns across the vast land—even all the way across the Bering Strait and into Alaska—then part of Russia. In reality, just like the Spanish, the Russians had their sights set on colonizing California. When the famous Swiss pioneer John Sutter arrived in northern California, he bought his land—Fort Ross—from Russia. Sutter is the man who established Sutter's Fort, present-day Sacramento.

Throughout the centuries, Russian civilization became intensely Christian. Russia and Orthodoxy became two sides of the same coin. And while there is always the risk of undesirable outcomes when the church and the state become enmeshed, one thing is clear: Russia became a profoundly Christian society.

Everything changed in the year 1917 when the Russian Empire collapsed and civil war broke out. The socialists—known as the Bolsheviks—emerged victorious. Their leader, Vladimir Lenin, was a convinced Marxist, and concluded that religion was detrimental to the state. Thus an intense persecution of Christianity began, and lasted all the way into the 1980s.

The scale of this anti-Christian persecution is mindboggling, especially during the four decades of brutal suppression under Stalin and Khrushchev, from 1922 to 1964. Hundreds of bishops and about 45,000 priests were killed during that time. The number of people martyred for their Christian faith has been estimated in the millions. Churches were closed or torn down, seminaries were emptied, and monasteries were shuttered.

And while some churches remained open, they were visited almost exclusively by *babushkas*—Russian grandmothers—who posed no threat to the paranoid government. In order to survive, most people kept their distance from the church, or what little remained of it. Practicing Christians typically kept their faith within them, as a private matter, so as not to trigger potentially violent attention from one of the myriad secret services patrolling the streets and infiltrating society.[4]

One famous victim of the oppression was the 1970 Nobel Prize in Literature recipient, Aleksandr Solzhenitsyn. Solzhenitsyn was born into the havoc of the Russian Revolution, in 1918. His writings lifted the curtain on the injustices happening in his nation throughout the long years of the Soviet Union. In books such as *The Gulag Archipelago*, *Cancer Ward*, and *In the First Circle*, he introduced Western readers to the totalitarianism that had swept him up and forced him into labor camps for several years, until he was eventually deported to the West. That deportation backfired on the Soviets when he became outspoken against the cruel inhumanity of the gulag system of internal exile, usually to the remote plains of Siberia.

In 1983, when receiving the prestigious Templeton

---

4. See Paul Mojzes, "Orthodoxy under Communism," in *Twentieth-Century Global Christianity*, ed. Mary Farrell Bednarowski (Minneapolis: Fortress Press, 2008), 138–55.

Award, Solzhenitsyn explained his interpretation of the events that had traumatized his nation:

If I were asked today to formulate as concisely as possible the main cause of the ruinous Revolution that swallowed up some sixty million of our people, I could not put it more accurately than to repeat: Men have forgotten God; that's why all this has happened.[5]

Solzhenitsyn's writings denounced the gulag system and humanized the prisoners who served in it. For example, he wrote of prisoners who were willing to risk everything just to have a few more minutes in front of a fire in Siberia's bitterly cold winter. He wrote of the loneliness of the isolation cell. He described the long, freezing winds that overcame many prisoners, and the sweet taste of a cigarette that could bring joy to the heart. He gave dignity to these millions of souls whose lives were entirely forgotten, wasted in service to that damned, reprehensible cause.[6]

The Communists stripped the church of its land and property. Russian icons—holy paintings of saints—were publicly desecrated. As atheistic propaganda increased, the government's mockery of Christianity intensified. Even inconsequential parishes in small towns were closed and priests deported due to the fear that clergy might hold some sway

---

5. See the transcript of Solzhenitsyn's 1983 Templeton address at http://www.roca.org/OA/36/36h.htm.
6. See Michael Kaufman, "Solzhenitsyn, Literary Giant Who Defied Soviets, Dies at 89," *New York Times*, 4 August 2008, located at http://www.nytimes.com/2008/08/04/books/04solzhenitsyn.html.

among their flocks. Crucially, the government severed all lines of communication within the church by closing the Orthodox Church's vast media empire, including all newspapers, journals, and publishing houses. Virtually unable to communicate with one another, the churches fell silent. Church leadership suddenly lost all control and in some cases the church even turned against itself.[7]

During the persecution, Russian church leaders disagreed over how to handle the catastrophic developments that had shaken their institutions. While virtually all clergy suddenly became enemies of the state, there were times when priests and even bishops swore loyalty to the regime in order to prevent further destruction. Obviously this caused hard feelings; some felt their clergy had betrayed Christ by joining with the atheists.

If the goal was to cripple Russian Orthodoxy, the socialists succeeded in virtually every way. Funding for the churches, seminaries, and clergy completely ceased. This impacted the church immediately, as formal theological and pastoral education was extinguished. Influential clergymen who might take a stand were removed from their posts and often sent to work in the gulag.

The darkest period of Stalin's persecution was in 1937–1938, a period known as the Great Terror, when hundreds of thousands of believers were either sent to the gulag or executed on the spot. In town after town, bishops and

---

7. On the church turning against itself, see Gregory Freeze, "From dechristianization to laicization: state, Church, and believers in Russia," *Canadian Slavonic Papers* 57, no. 1–2, 6–34 (2015), DOI: 10.1080/00085006.2015.1028723.

priests were lined up against a wall and shot. In Ulianovsk 267 believers were killed. In Sverdlovsk over one hundred clergy were shot, including thirteen bishops. Repeatedly, and without much afterthought, similar stories played out.[8]

By 1941, the Russian Orthodox Church was virtually dead. Only four bishops had managed to escape death or incarceration. Virtually all of the churches and institutions were shuttered or razed.[9] Russia was now home to absolutely zero monasteries, zero seminaries, and zero candidates for priesthood. All of the church-run homes for the aged were closed, all of the church schools were declared illegal, and all church charities ceased to exist.[10]

Surprisingly, during the Second World War, Stalin's fear of Hitler caused him to temporarily lift the persecution of Christians, as he needed every single person possible to resist the Nazis, including the beleaguered Christians. But when Stalin finally died in 1953, Khrushchev ratcheted up the persecution once again. By the end of the Khrushchev period, Russian Orthodoxy was a mere shadow of itself.[11]

In spite of massive destruction, the remaining faithful found outlets for their Orthodox faith. We must here make a distinction between the terms "dechurching" and "dechristianizing." Although the institution of the church had been

8. Freeze, "From dechristianization to laicization," 15.

9. Freeze, "From dechristianization to laicization," 15.

10. Timothy Ware, *The Orthodox Church: New Edition* (New York: Penguin, 1997), 162.

11. See Scott Kenworthy, "Russia and Eastern Europe," in *The Wiley-Blackwell Companion to World Christianity*, ed. Lamin Sanneh and Michael McClymond (Oxford: John Wiley & Sons, 2016), 505–6.

crushed, committed believers found alternative venues for their worship of the Lord, whether in cemetery chapels, underground churches, or even by taking secret pilgrimages to sites once considered holy in Orthodoxy.[12]

What is so surprising about the Russian persecution is not so much the scale of its destruction, or even the millions of deserters who were merely trying to save their own lives. What is truly astounding is how some people remained faithful to Christ, even during a completely hopeless situation, where a Christian was deemed to be an imbecile at best, and a traitor—worthy of horrific punishment—at worst.

Orthodox theologian Timothy Ware once wrote that these fires of persecution in fact "purified" the Russian Orthodox Church. In his view, the church was "cleansed of worldly elements" and "freed from the burden of insincere members who had merely conformed outwardly for social reasons."[13]

Russia had become a nation of martyrs, and as in other eras of church history, the church emerged stronger, more beautiful, and more pure than before. The apostle Peter wrote something very similar during a time of persecution in the first century of the faith:

In all this you greatly rejoice, though now for a little while you may have had to suffer grief in all kinds of trials. These have come so that the proven genuineness of your faith—of greater worth than gold, which perishes

12. Freeze, "From dechristianization to laicization," 16.
13. Ware, *The Orthodox Church*, 148.

even though refined by fire—may result in praise, glory and honor when Jesus Christ is revealed. (1 Peter 1:6–7)

Indeed Russians today notice the parallels. Although persecuted with unspeakable brutality, the blood of the martyrs watered the seeds of the church. In a strange twist, Russia's persecution is interpreted as a profound blessing—a wondrous opportunity for God's people to demonstrate their tenacious faithfulness.

When the Soviet Union collapsed, the Russian Orthodox Church began to be rebuilt on that bloody ground. Land that had been used for executions of priests now served as foundations for churches and monasteries to rise up. Where atheism was announced over loudspeakers, the gospel is now being heralded. Where Christ had been slain, he now resurrects in power and glory. For example, the Sretensky Monastery in Moscow "served as a killing ground in Stalin's time" but is now, once again, "a cinematically perfect vision of Orthodoxy."[14]

Russia's revolution, this time around, has taken on an entirely different character than the anti-religious Bolshevik Revolution of 1917. Indeed what is happening today is very good news. Christ has risen in Russia. Christ has risen indeed.

The Resurrection of Christianity in Russia

When Mikhail Gorbachev announced a policy of *glasnost*, or openness, to the Russian people in the 1980s, the Russian

14. Kishkovsky, "Russians See Church and State Come Closer."

Orthodox Church was immediately impacted. In just three decades nearly a thousand monasteries have sprung up, full of monks and nuns.[15] Thousands of churches have reopened or are under construction. Publishing houses, schools, youth organizations, orphanages, prison ministries, and charities of all kinds have opened to serve the Russian public.

Initially the nation became flooded with Protestants and Catholics, eager to bring the gospel to a people starved for religious faith. But the Orthodox Church deeply resented this development, and the repercussions from those days are still being felt. Russia feels it should evangelize its own. Indeed the Kremlin recently approved "anti-terror" legislation that effectively stops non-Orthodox religions from evangelizing in Russia. Anyone who wants to preach is required to obtain a permit, or else face a penalty of between $780 and $15,500. Foreigners who violate the law will be deported.[16]

Americans may balk at this sort of regulation on religious expression, but the Russian religious landscape is so utterly different that comparison is difficult. Russian history over the last century was unpredictable and turbulent: from state-church to horrific persecution to religious tolerance. Russia is home to some Jews and Muslims and other faiths, but the vast majority of Russians (around 75 percent) are Orthodox.

15. Metropolitan Hilarion of Volokolamsk, "The Voice of the Church Must Be Prophetic," *The Ecumenical Review* 65, no. 4 (December 2013). This article was actually delivered as a lecture for the World Council of Churches gathering in Busan, South Korea, in 2013. The transcript is located here: http://www.aoiusa.org/met-hilarion-the-voice-of-the-church-must-be-prophetic/.

16. Kate Shellnutt, "Russia's Newest Law: No Evangelizing Outside of Church," *Christianity Today*, 8 July 2016, located at http://www.christianitytoday.com/gleanings/2016/june/no-evangelizing-outside-of-church-russia-proposes.html.

Because of the Orthodox unity enjoyed by over three-fourths of the Russian people, comparing American Christianity to Russian Christianity is like comparing apples to oranges.

In America, our largest denomination is the Roman Catholic Church (21 percent), followed by Southern Baptists, who comprise less than 5 percent of the nation. But we have hundreds of other denominations, as well as many independent churches that are connected to no larger institution. American Christianity is bewilderingly diverse, and we have an *entirely* different history when it comes to religion's relationship to the government.

Russian Orthodoxy, however, has a long, thousand-year history of being closely connected to the state. And since the 1990s it has undergone a powerful rebirth. Since the Berlin Wall fell, it has become the world's second-largest denomination, after the Roman Catholic Church. Impressively, for the last three decades, the Russian Orthodox Church has opened three churches a day; nationally that's about a thousand per year. And there's no sign of reversal. Rather, the church's outreach and effectiveness seem to pick up steam annually.

Indeed Russia has become *proudly* Christian, recently celebrating its grand narrative of Christianization in the year 988 with a colossal statue of King Vladimir just one hundred yards outside the Kremlin walls in Moscow. Standing nearly sixty feet tall, the statue—erected in 2016—is hailed as "embodying Russia's core identity as a robust state built around Christian values."[17]

The church is not only back in Russia, it is thriving. Suddenly, in the blink of an eye, churches are packed not only with *babushkas* but with children being catechized, babies being baptized and christened, and entire families freely celebrating the Divine Liturgies of old. Soviet leaders in the 1970s would be very perplexed by how this all could have happened. Surely Lenin and Stalin are kicking and screaming in their graves.

Here's a key statistic that illustrates the dramatic changes happening. In 1989, 70 percent of Russians claimed to be atheists. In 2012, well over 70 percent of Russians declared themselves to be Orthodox Christians![18] The tables completely turned.

Recently I heard an important Russian church official deliver a lecture wherein he characterized the events of the last few decades as nothing less than a reversal of roles between Eastern Europe and Western Europe.[19] Throughout most of the twentieth century, he stated, Russia was atheist and Western Europe was full of Christians. But in the latter years of the twentieth century, the tables turned. Russia decided to welcome Christ into their culture again, while Western Europe underwent a process of secularization. Throughout most of the century, the Russians were closing churches left and right while the Western church thrived. But

---

17. Neil MacFarquhar, "A New Vladimir Overlooking Moscow," *New York Times*, 4 November 2016.
18. Kenworthy, "Russia and Eastern Europe," 506.
19. The official I heard speak was Metropolitan Hilarion. For more on this, see my book *To Whom Does Christianity Belong?* (Minneapolis: Fortress Press, 2015), 221–26.

now the complete opposite is happening. Western Europe closes their churches while Russia can't seem to build enough. Sometimes truth is stranger than fiction.

Recently, Dmitri Medvedev described the renaissance of the Orthodox Church as a "miracle."[20] Imagine that: the former President of Russia, speaking of the church in such glowing terms, even using the term "miracle"—a word that would not have been used by seven decades of Soviet atheists. Indeed, miracles require a God.

Today the Orthodox Church is firing on all cylinders. It runs publishing houses with several hundreds of religious journals published; it offers 3,500 websites; churches are popping up so quickly that the experts can't even keep track of them all.[21] As Christians we are witnesses to a rare event in the history of Christianity—an entire nation is returning to Christ.

Russian Christians will be the first to tell you, however, that there is still much work that remains to be done. While an unprecedented revival unfolds before our eyes, the truth is that most Russians were completely cut off from the church during Soviet times. They have no idea what's in the Bible. They don't understand church traditions and beliefs. They must learn very rudimentary things about the faith. They don't understand the church calendar or the liturgy. They don't attend church services with any kind of regularity simply because it is a practice entirely new to them. Building up

20. Freeze, "From dechristianization to laicization," 17.
21. Freeze, "From dechristianization to laicization," 17.

the Russian church will remain a work in progress, probably for decades to come, but at the very least Russians seem motivated to take on the task.

Pussy Riot, Constantine, and the Russian Church Today

In 2012, Russians were shocked when the punk band Pussy Riot rushed to the front of Moscow's Cathedral of Christ the Savior—one of the holiest sites in Russian Orthodoxy today—and performed a punk-prayer that was widely perceived as being blasphemous. They became famous for disrupting events—such as the Sochi Olympics—in order to make a point public. Outspoken in favor of LGBT rights and feminism, their approach is to jar the public through obscene lyrics and in-your-face methods. The group has received praised in the Western media for their songs of protest against Putin and his close relationship with the Orthodox Church. In Russia, however, they have been roundly criticized. Two Pussy Riot members were charged with hooliganism for the cathedral performance and spent nearly two years in prison doing hard labor.

The Pussy Riot controversy illustrates key differences between Russia and America, especially when it comes to free speech. But it also casts light on how seriously Russians now take their faith. The original Cathedral of Christ the Savior was destroyed by Stalin so that he could build a colossal palace dedicated to the Soviet cause. That building was never completed. But the church was rebuilt there in the 1990s and is today considered an emblem of Christ's victory over atheism and Soviet oppression. Many Russians viewed the Pussy Riot performance as vile and inappropriate. It mocked the church, and trivialized the deep meaning that most Russians recognize in it.

Americans are comfortable with public protest to a degree most Russians would find objectionable. Russia is emerging from a truly painful, horrific era in their history, and their civilization is still reeling from those events. For most Russians, this is not the time for mocking the government, or blaspheming the church. These two institutions are transforming a once-beleaguered society, and Russians are thankful for them. Russians are fully cognizant of their society's fragility, and what terrible things can happen when chaos prevails. Many Russians felt the members of Pussy Riot were pulling at the threads of a tapestry that could easily unravel again, and the band was consequently chastised for their actions.

When I think of Christianity's resurgence in Russia today, and its formal promotion by the state, I cannot help but think of the era of Emperor Constantine in the Roman Empire. Constantine is both loved and hated by theologians. On the one hand, he made Christianity legal. And for that he is praised. Christians were hunted and executed prior to his rule, and when he came to power he changed their situation immediately. In the Orthodox Church, Emperor Constantine is given the official title "Equal to the Apostles" because of the great favor he bestowed on Christianity. His conversion to Christianity was the icing on the cake. In the minds of Christians, the once-evil Roman Empire became Christian virtually overnight. They praised God for sending Constantine. And the persecutions ceased.

Some Russians seem to think they have found their Constantine in the decisions being made by Vladimir Putin. Not only has he stabilized Russia's economy, he also signifies a measure of dignity being returned to the land, the people, and its society in general. More importantly for the church, Putin has given it a green light and is avidly encouraging its rise. And the Russian people are reciprocating by investing themselves into their church, revitalizing it in creative and truly marvelous ways. They are beginning to hold their heads high again, and the Russian Orthodox Church is one of the great beneficiaries of this newfound confidence.

On the other hand, some Christians today see Constantine's era as the beginning of something really regrettable. Suddenly the church was virtually indistinguishable from the state. No more martyrs. Everybody was a Christian, at least in name. It wasn't long after Constantine's death that heretics were even hunted down and killed for *not being Christian enough*! Thus many Christians view Constantine as the person who watered down the faith and led us into a long Dark Age of corruption in the church.

It is far too early to say how all of this will affect Russian Christianity over the long term. It would truly be a shame if Russia became a totalitarian Christian state, where nonbelievers were persecuted, as happened shortly after Constantine. On the opposite end of the spectrum, however, it is also possible that another old-guard leader with Communist and atheist sympathies could rise to power. Personally, I think the former is more plausible than the latter, but this is Russia, and extreme volatility has characterized the nation for a century now.

For the time being, however, Russians are returning to Christ in ways that are both surprising and beautiful. In recent memory, priests were shot, believers were imprisoned, churches were destroyed, and a cloud of fear enveloped those who professed the name of Jesus. But lately, the exact reverse has happened. Christians are respected again, men are encouraged to join the priesthood, believers have the freedom to live their faith openly, and churches are being built on a scale unprecedented—perhaps not since the days of Constantine have we seen so much church construction. Monasteries are full of eager young men, desirous of the contemplative life. Laypeople are devoting their time and money to restoring old churches that were decommissioned during the long Soviet era.

Recently I read a story of laypeople working hard to restore their old church in a Russian village called Trubetskoye. The villagers hold charity fairs to raise money for their old church that had been left to ruin during the days of Communism. They allow stalls for people to sell their baked goods, old books, and art to locals and visitors from surrounding towns. The idea of their church's renovation actually came from a seventy-five-year-old retired engineering professor named Elina Loginova. She has done heroic work trying to help the village understand something of their roots, their past, and what their community used to be. Her research revealed that the church was a central part of their community until the Bolsheviks took control of their village in 1918. Ms. Loginova spearheads the fundraising efforts, and the villagers have rallied around her. At the most recent fair she spoke lovingly to her neighbors: "I have only one thing to say, thank you, thank you, thank you."[22]

In town after town, similar scenes are unfolding as Russians come together to piece together their broken churches. The Russian Orthodox Church, well-to-do philanthropists, and funds from the state are all helping to rebuild a parish infrastructure that was in tatters just two decades ago. Russians rally around their old churches in touching ways, such as donating old icons that somehow escaped the purges. They offer their time, their money, and perhaps most of all, their presence. The movie *Field of Dreams* made famous the notion that "if you build it they will come." That is what is happening in town after town and village after village in Russia.

Let us give credit where credit is due. It was not a given that Russia would bounce back like this. Russia is huge, easily the largest country in the world. Spanning eleven time zones, it is a wonder how this nation has managed to avoiding splitting into several countries. There was no guarantee that the nation would emerge intact. Nor was it certain that the Orthodox Church would play such a key role in Russia's turnaround. But it unmistakably has.

22. Alison Smale, "Restoring Old Churches Inspires a New Philanthropy in Russia," *New York Times*, 9 August 2016, located at https://www.nytimes.com/2016/08/10/world/europe/restoring-old-churches-inspires-a-new-philanthropy-in-russia.html?_r=0.

Russian identity took a beating over the last century. Their society was hijacked by a form of socialism that lifted up its own leaders as gods while brutally punishing any who disagreed. And while they defeated the Nazis, they proved susceptible to many of the same flaws that made the Nazis so detestable. Without a doubt Soviet Russia achieved great things in the latter half of the twentieth century: an illustrious space program, excellent education system, superb military, and world-class athletes. But it all came at a terrible cost. Their people were not free. Many of them even went hungry. Like a huge Ponzi scheme, the system was destined to collapse eventually. And it did. Adding insult to injury, the only way out of its malaise was for Russia to adopt the openness and the capitalism of its own worst enemies.

But Russia is rebuilding its identity today, and the Orthodox Church is at the center of the reconstruction. The nation has pinned its hopes to Christianity—precisely the opposite approach taken by Western Europe. Indeed, Russia is in many ways defining itself over against the decadence and moral relativism it perceives in the West. In its own mind it has traded places with Western Europe. It is transforming itself into a Christian society as Western Europe slowly drifts away from its Christian roots.[23] Even Joseph Ratzinger, the recent pope, lamented the growing relativism of Western society in his important book with a most revealing title: *Without Roots.*[24]

---

23. For an excellent article on the impact of the church on Russia today, see Larissa Andreeva and Scott Kenworthy, "Russia," in the *Worldmark Encyclopedia of Religious Practices*, 2nd ed. (Farmington Hills, MI: Gale, 2015).

Russia has unleashed the power of the church in a way that we in the West simply cannot comprehend due to our value of the separation of church and state. For example, for the first time in its history, the Russian Orthodox Church has established Christian universities funded mainly by wealthy businessmen who have literally bought into what is happening in their country. They see it as their patriotic duty to support the church because it is making a positive difference in their society: social outreach to the vulnerable, drug rehabilitation, hospice care, the arts, children's healthcare (such as programs for autism), and more. One expert put it this way: "The Church has reminded Russians of the immensity of the Bolshevik crimes against the nation and the need for national repentance and renewal."[25]

In theological parlance, Russia is adopting a kingdom theology approach, and is rejecting the separation model pioneered by the United States. It is using the playbook of medieval Christianity—a partnership between church and state. In America, we are a relatively religious people, but we denounce the enmeshment of church and state as being somehow un-American. Russia almost flaunts its pro-church model of social reform. Indeed the Russian government is *relying* on the church as a critical partner to achieve its strategic aims for the country.

Russian Orthodox Christianity has a history that we should

24. Joseph Ratzinger (Pope Benedict XVI), *Without Roots: The West, Relativism, Christianity, Islam* (New York: Basic Books, 2006).
25. See John Burgess, *Holy Rus': The Rebirth of Orthodoxy in the New Russia* (New Haven: Yale University Press, 2017), 80, 12.

appreciate. It has produced some truly important Christian thinkers such as Dostoyevsky and Solzhenitsyn. And although he was excommunicated from the church, there is no doubt that one of the greatest novelists of all time—Leo Tolstoy—was profoundly shaped by the Orthodox faith.[26] A renaissance of faith is dramatically changing Russian society, and those of us who profess Christ should notice a powerful lesson here: even when the future of Christianity looks grim, there is no limit on what God can accomplish—even against seemingly impossible odds.

Christianity is rising in Russia, even if it is a form of Christianity that we in the West are unfamiliar with. And for that we should be grateful. The gospel changes lives. And the gospel is being unleashed in this nation of 150 million souls. For decades Russia was a story of repression, of militant atheism, and of misery. But that is all changing, and it is accompanied by Christianity's sudden change of fortune in a nation that we never expected.

Who could possibly have imagined just a generation ago that in only a matter of years we would be talking about the revival of Christian faith in the heartland of the Soviet Union? But here we are. In Russia, Christianity has risen. And as they say in the Orthodox liturgy around Easter time: Christ has risen indeed.

---

26. In 2010, the Russian Orthodox Church reaffirmed its excommunication of Tolstoy in 2001, based on the fact that Tolstoy effectively excommunicated himself. This is a source of longstanding controversy and great regret in Russia. See http://www.pravoslavie.ru/english/42983.htm.

3

The United States: Is Christianity Dying or Thriving?

Okay, deep breath. I want to tell you a story that is very personal for me, but it illustrates what I'm trying to communicate in this chapter.

I grew up in Portales, New Mexico, and attended a little Church of Christ in the town that to this day is healthy, loving, and full of good people. But I must confess that in my youth I didn't take my faith very seriously. I was baptized at age eleven, and attended church services regularly with my parents. My religion, however, was sports with a large helping of theater on the side. Christianity was something I *did*, not something that I *was*.

But then came 1992. I was nineteen years old, emotionally broken, and without any direction for my life. I graduated from high school in 1991 with good grades and lots going for me. But within a year my life utterly fell apart. I went off to college to play tennis, but quickly realized I was not going to be the next Andre Agassi. My grades plummeted because I thought more about tennis and nightlife than I did about my academic standing. Then to top it all off my girlfriend—my high school sweetheart—dumped me. Forlorn and confused, I could barely muster an appetite for several weeks. Adulthood was going to be difficult for me.

At first I turned to the wrong things, you know, all those vices that eighteen- and nineteen-year-olds turn to. Predictably, things didn't get any better. I was just racking up more problems for myself.

But then one night while in my bedroom there at my parents' house, my pensive gaze somehow landed on a bookshelf to notice a red hardback book titled *Six Hours One Friday: Anchoring to the Cross* by Max Lucado. Pulling it from the shelf, I thought I'd check it out.

Lucado is one of America's best-selling authors, and, looking back, it is easy for me to see why. It is not high-brow theology. Rather, Lucado writes for average Christian people who need to be reminded that there is a God, that he sent his son Jesus Christ, and that each person has potential. More than anything, I began to understand that God wants to get to know me, personally. For some reason I had never really thought about that.

It brought me to tears and convinced me that I was on the wrong path. I needed to reconnect with that faith I had completely taken for granted. In truth, that was the moment when I began to love God with my heart and with my soul. Strangely, I had never really done that before.

So I enrolled at Lubbock Christian University and began taking theology classes. I befriended another theology student named John Williamson and we began praying in our dorm rooms each evening and having Bible study breakfasts every Saturday morning. I kept a tiny green Gideon Bible in my back pocket to pull out during any lulls in my schedule. I began tapping into God's word for daily sustenance, and my faith began to deepen and strengthen exponentially. My life was turning around! I actually had value! It excited me that maybe I, even I, could perhaps help others!

I decided to train for pastoral ministry and make the study of Christianity my life's work. And so that's what I do now, a quarter-century later.

I can't say Max Lucado's book was responsible for everything that happened, but it was certainly a pivot. For several years I read everything written by him. When a new book came out, I would rush to the Christian bookstore to get my hands on it. I listened to him on the radio. I longed to meet this man who wrote a book that, truly, gave me some hope at a point when I was miserable, wallowing in failure.

A couple of years after my turnaround I visited San Antonio and attended Oak Hills Church where Lucado was and still is the minister. I was not accustomed to large churches, and there were hundreds of people there listening to the man who had changed my life. After services, with sweaty palms and a palpitating heart, I stood in line to shake his hand. I was one of many, but when my turn came, I looked him right in the eye and said, "Hello Mr. Lucado. It is really great to meet you. I really enjoyed your message." He smiled and shook my hand. He had no idea of the important role he had played in my life. He was gracious, and thanked me for coming. I felt like I had just shaken hands with an American president.

Secular California . . . or Not

But that was in Texas, where Christianity thrives, and where America's largest congregation (Joel Osteen's Lakewood Church with around 44,000 weekly) stands as a testament to the great power and reach of American Christianity today.

Today, however, I live in California, one of the least religious states in America.[1] Known for Silicon Valley, Hollywood, dark tans, and plastic surgery, our state is associated with glitz, glamor, and beautifully sculpted bodies. We focus on the here and now: muscle cars, surfing, Disneyland, and our eternal sunshine. Christianity does not appear to be thriving here.

In reality, however, nothing could be further from the truth. Christianity booms in my state today; it just depends on where you look.

Let's set our sights on Los Angeles for a minute, my neck of the woods. L.A. is home to the largest Roman Catholic diocese in the United States, with a beautiful and massive cathe-

---

1. California is ranked as the eleventh least-religious U.S. state according to Pew Research, based on the percentage of respondents who claimed in 2014 that religion is "very important" or "somewhat important" to them. See http://www.pewforum.org/religious-landscape-study/state/alabama/#importance-of-religion-by-state.

dral that fills up regularly on weekends. L.A. is also home to America's largest Pentecostal denomination—the Church of God in Christ—a majority black denomination led by Bishop Charles Blake. Pasadena, just outside of L.A., is home to Fuller Theological Seminary, America's largest institution for the training of Christian clergy.[2]

Greater Los Angeles, best known for its film industry and beaches, happens to be the place where Billy Graham skyrocketed to fame in 1949 with his pivotal L.A. Crusade that launched his public ministry and made him a household name. It landed him on the front page of nearly every major American newspaper and the cover of many magazines, since he was backed by both William Randolph Hearst and Henry Luce—the great media tycoons of the age. One could make a good case that America's unique style of evangelicalism, which survives to the present, is in many ways a direct consequence of that incredibly successful eight-week revival. The L.A. Crusade set in motion the modern evangelical movement and placed Billy Graham at the helm.

Furthermore, southern California is home to some of the most vibrant churches and Christian movements in America today, including Calvary Chapel, Vineyard, Saddleback (with its famous pastor Rick Warren), L.A. Dream Center, Reality, and Mosaic. New Christian movements continue to rise up here in California.

One such group began in Sacramento and is called Jesus

2. See the 2016–2017 Annual Data Tables for the Association of Theological Schools, located at http://www.ats.edu/uploads/resources/institutional-data/annual-data-tables/2016-2017-annual-data-tables.pdf.

Culture. Founded in 2014, it is now bursting with well over two thousand members and no signs of stopping. Jesus Culture is an unapologetically charismatic church, focusing on healing people and families in the name of Christ. Many claim their bodies and souls have been healed by God through its ministries. Their message is touching people's lives, making a major impact all over this supposedly secular state.[3]

Jesus Culture actually sprang out of Bethel Church, a large ministry based in Redding, California. Bethel has about nine thousand attendees per Sunday and a $9-million operating budget. It operates an international ministry known as iBethel as well as the Bethel School of Supernatural Ministry for those who wish to enter revivalist and healing ministries. It currently has more than two thousand students from fifty-seven countries. Bethel is also known for its vibrant music ministry, Bethel Music, which in 2016 placed a live worship album at number one on the iTunes album chart.[4]

Jesus Culture and Bethel Church are attached to a loosely organized movement with lofty ambitions to reconnect Americans with Christ. Known by scholars as Independent Network Charismatic (INC), this movement is "significantly changing the religious landscape in America—and its politics."[5] Several high-profile politicians have participated in

---

3. See Stephen Magagnini, "Musically driven Jesus Culture grows from California roots into global faith community," *The Sacramento Bee*, 19 March 2017, located at http://www.sacbee.com/entertainment/living/religion/article139557088.html. See the Jesus Culture website at https://jesusculture.com/about/.

4. Martyn Wendell Jones, "Cover Story: Inside the Popular, Controversial Bethel Church," *Christianity Today*, 24 April 2016, located at http://www.christianitytoday.com/ct/2016/may/cover-story-inside-popular-controversial-bethel-church.html?start=2.

their events, for example Rick Perry, Sarah Palin, Newt Gingrich, Bobby Jindal, and even Donald Trump when he was running for office.

In April 2016 this movement held a conference in Los Angeles Memorial Coliseum that attracted tens of thousands of people who prayed for the transformation of America and spent sixteen hours in healing sessions. The timing of their conference was strategic. It was commemorating the 110-year anniversary of the Azusa Street Revival in Los Angeles that gave birth to the modern Pentecostal Movement—a movement that now claims nearly half a billion Christians living primarily in the nations of the global south.[6]

INC Christianity is not so much about starting new churches or strengthening existing ones. Rather, it is more concerned with "transforming society through placing Christian believers in powerful positions in all sectors of society." It has real media savvy and excellent music, flashy websites, and well-organized funding techniques. It has been called "the fastest-growing Christian group in America and possibly around the world."[7]

The United States is full of these kinds of stories if we look beyond the headlines that typically emphasize the decline of Christianity in this nation.

Another INC church, the Kansas City–based International

5. Brad Christerson and Richard Flory, "How a Christian Movement Is Growing Rapidly in the Midst of Religious Decline," *The Conversation*, 17 March 2017, located at https://theconversation.com/how-a-christian-movement-is-growing-rapidly-in-the-midst-of-religious-decline-73507.

6. See the conference website at http://www.thecall.com/azusa.

7. Christerson and Flory, "How a Christian Movement Is Growing Rapidly."

House of Prayer (IHOP), has tens of millions of viewers who download massive amounts of video content—about a million hours per month.[8] IHOP's approach to faith is unabashedly charismatic: speaking in tongues, casting out demons, prophecy, being slain in the Holy Spirit, instant healing, shouting, you name it.[9] And one thing that is proving very favorable for this movement is that it is extremely attractive to young people. Millennials—people born in the 1980s and 1990s—flock to these kinds of churches. While many traditional American pastors struggle to woo Millennials their direction, the charismatic INC churches struggle to provide enough seats for them.

The philosophy of the INC movement is to create a trickle-down effect. They reach out to major players in business, entertainment, education, and media in hopes that those at the very top will come to Christ. In turn, that Christian influence will trickle down through these major organizations and eventually permeate American culture. Their goals are nothing less than cultivating peace, drawing people back to biblical morality, and achieving true social justice for all. Their theological agenda is kingdom-centered, that is, to bring heaven to earth just as Jesus prayed in the Lord's Prayer.[10]

8. Christerson and Flory, "How a Christian Movement Is Growing Rapidly."
9. See one of the IHOP websites: http://www.ihopeg.org/faq/.
10. Christerson and Flory, "How a Christian Movement Is Growing Rapidly."

False Alarm: America Is Not Turning Secular

Some people might dismiss these new forms of American Christianity as being mere last gasps for religion in the United States. According to this perspective, America is on the road to secularization. Despite revivals that might spring up here and there, the long perspective is clear: Christianity dies while science rises. And, so the argument goes, there seems not to be room for both. As one writer put it, "Every piece of social data suggests that those who favor faith and superstition over fact-based evidence will become the minority in this country by or before the end of this century." This same writer claims that in about a century, only 1 percent of Americans will identify as being Christian.[11]

This pessimistic perspective on the future of Christianity in America is not without its supporting arguments and evidence. But the fact that trends are headed in one direction doesn't mean that they will continue to do so forever. Events happen that change statistical trends all the time. One hundred years ago, no one would have believed that sub-Saharan Africa would soon become the center of the Christian world. Or that Brazil would soon become the nation with the most Pentecostals.

America, I argue, is not becoming more secular. In fact, some social science is showing that churches are as robust today as at any point in U.S. history. For example, sociologists

---

11. C. J. Werleman, "Atheists have their number," *Salon*, 25 March 2014, located at http://www.salon.com/2014/03/25/calling_the_christian_right_soon_you_will_be _outnumbered_partner/.

point out that in 1774, only 17 percent of Americans adhered to *any* religion. By 1990, fully 62 percent of Americans formally affiliated with a particular religion.[12]

And the numbers keep climbing. By 2007 around 70 percent of Americans claimed to "actually belong to a local church congregation."[13] Perhaps somewhat surprisingly, the percentage of American atheists has remained steady—around 4 percent—since the 1940s.

We've been told that atheism is growing rapidly, but that is untrue according to the numbers. Americans are today *far more religious* than they were when this nation was founded, and religious adherence in the U.S. might be going up, not down. It is true that people are not as committed to their specific denominations today, but it is far from clear that they have dropped faith altogether.

Pew Forum is one credible research outlet that deserves attention here. Their Religious Landscape surveys paint a picture of Christian decline that is routinely and widely reported in the American media. Thousands of pages of data have been compiled over the last several years, which, according to them, show that "the Christian share of the U.S. population is declining, while the number of U.S. adults who do not identify with any organized religion is growing."[14]

One of the pillars of the decline thesis has to do with the

---

12. Fenggang Yang, *Religion in China* (Oxford: Oxford University Press, 2012), 176. Yang uses the research of Roger Finke and Rodney Stark, *The Churching of America, 1776–1990: Winners and Losers in Our Religious Economy* (New Brunswick, NJ: Rutgers University Press, 1992).
13. Rodney Stark, *The Triumph of Christianity* (New York: HarperOne, 2011), 373.
14. "America's Changing Religious Landscape," *Pew Research Center*, 12 May 2015,

religious Nones—that group of people who say they have no religious affiliation. The individuals in this group claim to be agnostics, atheists, or nothing in particular. Perhaps the most often-highlighted statistic is this one: "35% of Millennials are Nones."[15] So the argument goes, if the Millennials are not attending church, then the future of religion looks very grim indeed. What people often forget, however, is that we tend to invest ourselves into religion more as we age.[16] If history is any indication, then over time Millennials will come back to church.

Millennials tend to prolong their adolescence much longer than previous generations. They get married later in life, they rely on their parents longer, and they take longer to settle. Whereas many Americans in the past wanted to start a family and purchase a home by their late twenties, many Millennials are still going to school, traveling, or just having fun being young.[17]

I like the quip by author Mary Eberstadt: "Children drive parents to church."[18] Her research shows that when couples start having children they contemplate bigger issues like

located at http://www.pewforum.org/2015/05/12/americas-changing-religious-landscape/.

15. Michael Lipka, "A closer look at America's rapidly growing religious 'nones'," *Pew Research Center*, 13 May 2015, located at http://www.pewresearch.org/fact-tank/2015/05/13/a-closer-look-at-americas-rapidly-growing-religious-nones/.

16. See Robert Putnam and David Campbell, *American Grace* (New York: Simon & Schuster, 2010), 26. They write, "The old are more religious than the young."

17. See Jonathan Vespa, "The Changing Economics and Demographics of Young Adulthood: 1975–2016," *United States Census Bureau*, April 2017, located at https://www.census.gov/content/dam/Census/library/publications/2017/demo/p20-579.pdf.

18. Mary Eberstadt, *How the West Really Lost God* (West Conshohocken, PA: Templeton, 2013), 95.

morality and virtue, and where to go to instill good values into their kids. In America, that place is usually down at the local church.

Eberstadt is fully aware, however, that as Americans wait longer to marry, and as they produce fewer and fewer children, the natural consequence will be a Christianity that is less vibrant—with smaller Sunday school enrollments. Of course that doesn't bode well for the future of the faith.

Eberstadt confirms what a number of scholars have demonstrated through the years: there is an obvious link between religiosity and fertility. Deeply religious families have more children. And large families tend to be more religious than smaller ones. Globally this is also true. For example, Africans—with a fertility rate of five children per woman—tend to be comparatively more religious.[19] We can contrast these figures with Europeans, who have the lowest fertility rates in the world, and consequently, very low participation rates in their churches.

In my view, these data suggest that religion is in a good position statistically. As more children are born into large and therefore religious families, they will likely raise their children to be religious.

I was intrigued by a recent biological study that argued the future of humanity will be religious since larger families are generally more religious. Further, they showed that religiosity and fertility tend to be inherited traits from the parents. In

19. Dyron Daughrity, *The Changing World of Christianity* (New York: Peter Lang, 2010), 93.

other words, if our parents raise us religiously, we are more likely to become religious adults. Similarly, if we come from a large family, we are more likely to bring more children into the world.[20]

Yet, fertility rates are falling in much of the world. China—the world's most populous nation—has a very low fertility rate (1.66 births per woman), even lower than America's (1.86). Europe's fertility rate is the lowest in the world. A recent study shows that even in Latin America the fertility rates are falling dramatically.[21] Ostensibly, the global population should be shrinking. Instead, it is growing because the nations with the highest fertility rates—twenty-nine of the top thirty most fertile nations are in Africa—are able to offset the nations with lower fertility, leading to an overall increase in the global population.[22]

Here's a key conclusion that can be drawn from all of this research: as American and European fertility rates decline, reliance on foreign labor will necessitate a steady flow of immigrants. And since these immigrants tend to have higher fertility and greater religiosity, the religious population will grow much faster than the secular one. Thus, as we are now

20. Lee Ellis, Anthony Hoskin, Edward Dutton, Helmuth Nyborg, "The Future of Secularism: A Biologically Informed Theory Supplemented with Cross-Cultural Evidence," in *Evolutionary Psychological Science* (8 March 2017), located at https://link.springer.com/article/10.1007/s40806-017-0090-z#enumeration.
21. See "Autumn of the patriarchs," *The Economist*, 1 June 2013, located at http://www.economist.com/news/americas/21578710-traditional-demographic-patterns-are-changing-astonishingly-fast-autumn-patriarchs.
22. See CIA World Factbook, "2016 Total Fertility Rate," located at https://www.cia.gov/library/publications/the-world-factbook/rankorder/2127rank.html.

witnessing, immigration to the U.S. and Western Europe will boost religiosity.

This is good news for religious folk. And it is particularly good news for American Christians, since the vast majority of immigrants to the U.S. are from Latin America—the region of the world containing the highest percentage of Christians.

In particular, Roman Catholics in America have every reason to be optimistic about the future of their church because the lion's share of these Latin American immigrants are and will remain Catholic. And because of slightly higher fertility rates among Latinos, the Catholic population in America is growing at a faster rate than the general population.[23] Experts are already declaring that "the American Catholic Church is on its way to becoming a majority-Latino institution."[24]

Pew Research caused a stir recently when they forecasted that around the year 2060, Islam will surpass Christianity as the world's largest religion. Their predictions are based on "simple demographics"—that Muslims have very high fertility rates—far higher than any other religious group. In addition, Muslims are on average younger than other religious groups. The average age of Muslims worldwide is twenty-four, while the average age of all non-Muslims is thirty-two. Thus Islam is set to experience a major population boom over the coming decades.[25]

---

23. See Ann Schneible, "The Catholic Church grew faster than the global population in past decade," *Catholic News Agency*, 9 March 2016, located at http://www.catholic-newsagency.com/news/the-catholic-church-grew-faster-than-the-global-population-last-year-79664/.
24. Putnam and Campbell, *American Grace*, 17.
25. Michael Lipka and Conrad Hackett, "Why Muslims are the world's fastest growing

Islam and Christianity will remain the largest religions of the world for the foreseeable future. But what is becoming clearer and clearer is that the *kind* of Christianity that is going to continue to proliferate is not the kind of Christianity many of us in America are used to. We are going to see less and less of the mainline Protestant forms of Christianity. Indeed statisticians tell us that America has more religious Nones than members of mainline Protestant churches.[26]

What is thriving in America today is Latino Catholicism, Pentecostalism, and more charismatic forms of the faith. Rarely do you see an Episcopal congregation bursting at the seams to the point that it must plant new churches. But this scenario is commonplace in Baptist, Pentecostal, and charismatic churches.

For example, Rick Warren's Saddleback Church began in southern California in 1980. Today it has sixteen California campuses and four international campuses, in Germany, Argentina, Hong Kong, and the Philippines.[27] They are planning many more campuses, and their virtual services are downloaded all over the world.

Another example of a thriving evangelical movement is the Willow Creek network of churches based in Illinois. Begun in 1975 by pastor Bill Hybels, they now have seven congregations scattered around Chicago and they conduct Global

religious group," *Pew Research Center*, 6 April 2017, located at http://www.pewresearch.org/fact-tank/2017/04/06/why-muslims-are-the-worlds-fastest-growing-religious-group/.

26. Putnam and Campbell, *American Grace*, 17.
27. See the Saddleback website: https://saddleback.com/visit/locations.

Leadership Summits in 125 nations (in fifty-nine languages) all over the world.[28]

Even if Christianity is on the decline in the United States, there is ample evidence to indicate that those American Christians who are still active are sowing a lot of seeds, and reaping a global harvest that will not soon dissipate.

Changes in American Christianity

I don't think America is turning secular on a broad scale. I think American Christianity is simply changing, and we're struggling to understand what exactly is happening.

For instance, I'm not convinced that Millennials are as secular as people say they are. They may return to church as they age and start families of their own.

The hippies of the 1960s are all grown up now, and many of them are today rather stable, settled, churchgoing people—a far cry from their Woodstock days of mushrooms and free love. As our setting in life changes, we think differently about things.

Recently I read a fascinating piece about how the hippie generation did an about-face in only a couple of decades. In the 1960s they marched and protested in ways this country had never seen before, and they were almost all Democrats. But in the 1980s they "voted overwhelmingly for Ronald Reagan." The writer reminded us that "what seems permanent can become fleeting." One can scarcely predict the

---

28. See the Willow Creek website: https://www.willowcreek.com/about/summit.asp.

future based on the present, especially when we account for the changes that occur in people over time.[29]

It is misguided to think that just because Millennials seem unplugged from faith, they will remain so forever. I doubt that the majority of young people have *ever* been strongly religious in America.

American historians tell us that Christianity in this nation has always ebbed and flowed. The Puritans were very religious. Their children not so much. But then the first Great Awakening occurred in the 1730s with the preaching of Jonathan Edwards and George Whitefield. Christianity reached new heights during the era. But then things cooled down again.

The Second Great Awakening renewed Christianity with massive revivals that took place all across the nation, notably at the famous Cane Ridge Revival in Kentucky in 1801, which drew thousands of pioneers together for a time of profoundly ecumenical worship. Then the fires of renewal began to smolder again until the great Azusa Street Revival in 1906 unleashed Pentecostal Christianity all across the globe—a process that continues unabated.

In 1966 the cover of *Time* magazine famously asked the question "Is God Dead?," much to the chagrin of Christians. But once again, reports of the death of God—and of Christianity—were greatly exaggerated. Certainly the 1960s and 1970s were a time of protest, unprecedented freedom, and

29. David Leonhardt, "Why Teenagers Today May Grow Up Conservative," *New York Times*, 8 July 2014, located at https://www.nytimes.com/2014/07/08/upshot/why-teenagers-may-be-getting-more-conservative.html?_r=0.

broad social change, but in spite of those movements, God did not die, and religion did not go away. It changed. The way we thought about God changed.

Besides, many of the protests of that era were profoundly religious. Some of our preachers, like Martin Luther King Jr., taught us that protest anchored in Jesus's teaching could be profoundly Christian, and could lead us to greater justice, greater respect, and a more authentic Christian witness.

No, God did not die in the sexual revolution. God did not go away when the U.S. went to war with Vietnam. God did not abandon America when we put people on the moon and peered into other galaxies. It is quite possible that Christianity was *aided* by all of these events.

As technology moves rapidly around us and sometimes through us, we also have to be prepared to explain our faith in fresh and innovative ways. This is precisely where many churches falter. They lose touch with society around them and quite suddenly become irrelevant. But other churches adjust to these changes with remarkable fluidity. And still other churches rise up out of nowhere.

All things considered, the Christian faith adapted to the social and technological changes of the last few decades quite effectively. And rather than wilt and die, the church dove in headfirst and offered many responses to help guide people through the shifts that were happening around them at breakneck speed. The Roman Catholic Church held a huge council in the 1960s—Vatican II—aimed specifically at making the church relevant in a society that had seemingly passed it up. The evangelical movement rose up in the 1980s with its thousands of megachurches. The emerging church movements of the last twenty years—geared specifically to helping Christians adjust to society's changing ethos—brought others back into the fold.

Rob Bell is probably the most well-known emergent church figure due to his bestselling book *Love Wins* as well as his work with Oprah Winfrey. He is doing what pioneering thinkers in our rich Christian heritage have always done—they help us to see things differently, even in the face of criticism.

Some of the great Christian pioneers of the past were demonized or even killed for their "strange" teachings: Anselm, Aquinas, Huss, Wycliffe, Savonarola, Luther, Wesley, and MLK. During their day, all of these individuals attracted condemnation by many Christians around them.

Anselm was exiled twice. Aquinas was condemned before he was canonized. Huss was burned at the stake. Wycliffe's bones were dug up and burned after condemnation. Savonarola was hanged and burned. Luther was enemy number one of the Roman church for centuries. Wesley was blacklisted by the Church of England. MLK was shot and killed.

Yet all of these individuals stood for what they believed to be true; very few of us doubt their sincerity. Rather than sitting idly by, they took up the challenge to try and make a difference. Their goal was to apply the Christian faith anew, to think new thoughts, and to innovate.

And so here we are again. American Christianity faces a challenging future. Let's not be naïve enough to think Christianity won't respond competently to the cultural changes happening around us. Don't ever count out the church, especially the American church. It will adapt. It will look to the Bible, to the saints, and to the rich heritage of the past to provide us with gifts and tools for moving forward.

Change the World or Withdraw from It

In 1995 I began attending seminary at Abilene Christian University right smack in the heart of Texas. One of the best courses I took dealt with how Christian theology relates to culture. One of our textbooks was the classic *Christ and Culture*, written by H. Richard Niebuhr—a theology professor at Yale from 1931 to 1962.

Anybody who has read *Christ and Culture* is aware of its clear presentation of how Christians have related to culture throughout history. Niebuhr describes five different approaches.

First, some Christians reject culture. These are the radicals who turn their backs on the surrounding culture, usually because it has become overly sinful. There is a clear line in the sand: you are a Christian or you are not a Christian. We can think of monks, or perhaps a more American example, the Amish.

The second group Niebuhr describes as "accommodationists." These people "harmonize Christ and culture." Niebuhr says we can think of liberal Protestantism here—the type of

Protestant Christianity that dominated in America up until the mid-twentieth century.[30]

The third group is labeled "the church of the center." These people try to avoid extremes. They don't want to be too progressive, but they don't want to be seen as radicals, either. They prefer to fly under the radar, calling themselves Christians, but not creating too much of a fuss. Niebuhr calls them "cultural Christians." The problem, he argues, is that there is little distinction between these individuals and non-Christians. Yes, they claim to be Christians, but there is nothing "distinctively Christian" about them.[31]

The fourth group is what Niebuhr calls "the dualists." But what he has in mind is Christian conservatism. These people are decidedly Christian, but they tend to admire the past to an unhealthy degree. If it were up to these conservatives, they may have held onto slavery or forbidden the emancipation of women. He cites the apostle Paul and Martin Luther as being of this ilk. They were true Christians, but didn't think to challenge social norms that were obviously unfair to certain people.[32]

The fifth group is called the "transformers of culture." These people try to transform society. They are incredibly engaged in society. They are motivated by Christian faith to make changes that will benefit people. They boldly oppose the social ills that they deem sinful. They try to transform

30. H. Richard Niebuhr, *Christ and Culture* (New York: Harper & Row, 1951), 83–84.
31. Niebuhr, *Christ and Culture*, 143.
32. See especially Niebuhr, *Christ and Culture*, 188.

corrupted social institutions so that they will better reflect God's intentions for humanity.

Niebuhr seems to prefer the last group, but he warns that none of these categories are watertight. With all kinds of crossover between them, it is erroneous to think there is one correct option among the five.

Since its publication in 1951, *Christ and Culture* has offered Christians a helpful way of thinking about how we should relate to our society. I think it is reasonable to conclude that most Christians fit somewhere in the middle. We do our best to live our faith but we don't want to stick out and call attention to ourselves as being extremists either on one side or the other. But perhaps it is helpful to look at the extremes in order to understand better how we fit in.

So let us discuss examples of the two polar-opposite views in this discussion: the transformer/engagement approach versus the withdrawal approach. Some Christians choose to actively transform their society through full engagement, while others have a rejection mentality, arguing that Christians should withdraw from what they perceive to be widespread social decadence happening all around them.

The first response is that of full engagement. In this model, American Christians need to abide by a concept James Davison Hunter calls "faithful presence." They should be "faithfully present" in their culture, positioning themselves to change the world around them.[33]

---

33. Much of my argument here comes from James Davison Hunter, *To Change the World* (Oxford: Oxford University Press, 2010).

According to this view, committed Christians are not making much of an impact in the most prestigious and influential places. They have not impacted culture as much as they could have done because they rarely rise to the top in American society. If Christians want to truly make an impact in, say, journalism, they must aspire to the most prestigious journals and newspapers in their profession, rather than settling for second-tier journals or strictly Christian newspapers. A person in this camp would say it is a mistake to write only for like-minded Christians. Rather, you need to engage the broader, more secular society.

For example, Michael Luo is a Harvard-educated evangelical Christian who for years wrote and edited for the *New York Times*—probably America's most prestigious newspaper. In Luo's mind, America's most influential institutions often suffer from "a dearth of Christians." He argues that many of the reporters and editors at the *New York Times* don't understand the Christian worldview very well, which "can lead to bias seeping through in the way Christians are depicted." However, "you can't know what you don't know." Thus Luo wears his evangelical Presbyterian faith proudly at work in hopes that he might make some kind of impact on the very influential journalists that surround him at the peak of their profession.[34]

In the transformer/engagement view, many American

---

34. See Paul Glader, "Meet the Christian Reporter Climbing the Ladder at The New York Times," *Christianity Today*, 22 November 2013, located at http://www.christianitytoday.com/ct/2013/december/meet-christian-reporter-climbing-ladder-at-new-york-times.html.

Christians have mistakenly developed parallel institutions in their quest to be more devout. However, they have lost influence in society because nonreligious people don't take them very seriously. Think Christian novels, the Christian film industry, and Christian newspapers. These people have good intentions, but they don't change culture because they're merely preaching to the choir. By establishing *Christian* radio, *Christian* websites, and *Christian* newspapers, they negate their impact on anyone outside their own little social group.

Of course Christians will watch Christian films, but it is unlikely that a regular reader of the *New York Times* is going to set aside her Friday nights to watch the *Left Behind* movies or read Janette Oke novels.

By contrast, many Christians *are* going to watch *Star Wars* and *The Fast and the Furious*, and they're probably going to read the latest Dan Brown novel. In other words, the influence goes only one way. Christians end up getting influenced *by* secular culture, but they fail to have any influence on the wider world around them.

According to the transformer/engagement view, Christians need to aspire to make an impact in *mainstream* society. They should work to place their kids in MIT, Yale, and Harvard rather than just putting them into overtly Christian schools. They should try to write for the *New York Times* and make an impact on *America*, not just on conservative Christian America.

The second approach—withdrawal from society—is the exact opposite.[35] In this view, American culture is in crisis, and moral depravity abounds. This perspective asserts that the time has come for firmly committed Christians to reject their culture and to develop separate institutions. Not just parallel institutions, but a literal retreat into their own separate communities where they can keep some distance between their families and the outside world.

Many religious people have taken this stance throughout history. Around the time of Christ, the Dead Sea Scrolls community retreated to the caves of Qumran to escape what they perceived to be moral laxity in Israel. In the 500s, St. Benedict—the father of Western monasticism—established monasteries as Roman society was being overrun by barbarians. In the Middle Ages, St. Francis of Assisi famously sold everything he had and devoted himself to preaching the gospel and serving others in the name of Christ. In America we have our own examples such as the Amish, the Hutterites, and the Mormons who in their early years kept moving west until they settled in Salt Lake City—far away from the rest of the United States—in an attempt to escape persecution and establish a civilization of their own. In America's largest cities we have Hasidic Jewish neighborhoods where the ultra-Orthodox keep the world at bay.

I have a friend in Germany named Jutta Koslowski. She is an ordained Lutheran pastor and theologian. Around 2007

---

35. A recent book illustrates the withdrawal perspective extremely well: Rod Dreher, *The Benedict Option* (New York: Sentinel, 2017). David Brooks of the *New York Times* considers this book "the most discussed and important religious book of the decade." See "The Benedict Option," *New York Times*, 14 March 2017, located at https://www.nytimes.com/2017/03/14/opinion/the-benedict-option.html.

she and her family decided to withdraw to a religious community outside of Frankfurt and form a Christian community called Jesus Brotherhood.[36] They live in a former Cistercian convent at a place called Gnadenthal.

Jutta and her husband have several children, but the larger community consists of other families, as well as some celibate men and women. The entire group partakes in regular prayer, daily worship, morning celebration of the Lord's Supper, and a deep commitment among each member of the community to care for one another. Like many monasteries, they offer hospitality to guests, and produce much of their own food with an organic farm.

Jutta and her family have chosen to withdraw. But even in their case it is a struggle to keep her kids on the Christian path while the society around them is so secular. Even Jutta's own parents are at times a threat to their way of life because they just don't understand the need for Jutta and her husband to be so religious. When their kids travel to see their grandparents, they come home with many questions and critiques of the religious life. For instance, they wonder why it is important to pray before meals when virtually nobody around them—including their own grandparents—practices this strange ritual.

Jutta loves her religious community and she is thankful that they made the decision to withdraw. But homeschooling is illegal in Germany. There are no exceptions. So Jutta's chil-

36. See their website: http://www.jesus-bruderschaft.de/.

dren are being socialized in the secular schools, and it leads them to question the choices their parents have made.

The point here is this: even when a person or a community chooses to withdraw, it is almost impossible in today's world to sever the cord to larger society.

We can try to change our world, or we can withdraw from society in order to preserve our Christian faith. Both approaches have merit, presenting us with two viable solutions to a very difficult question: How should we respond to culture?

Some of us will choose to make a big splash wherever God places us, and, if possible, we will work our way up the ladder and influence more and more people in the name of Christ.

A few of us, however, will perceive our society as entering a long dark age, an era of malaise and decadence. If we want to save our own souls and the souls of those closest to us, then we will need to turn more deliberately toward the Christian faith and the solutions it has provided for centuries.

Despite sometimes dire predictions for the future of American Christianity, Pew Research paints a very Christian picture of today's America.[37] Over 70 percent of Americans self-identify as Christians. Less than 6 percent of Americans identify with all of the non-Christian religions combined. Only 3 percent of us are atheists. We often think of America as a diverse place. But religiously this is not so.

Americans are not abandoning Christianity. Rather, as a

---

37. See the ongoing Pew Research Center "Religious Landscape Study" at http://www.pewforum.org/religious-landscape-study/.

nation we are changing. And, consequently, we are changing the Christian faith in our land. So many changes have occurred over the last generation: gender roles, sexuality, family structure, the role of the clergy, ethnic diversification, the decline of the mainline and rise of the charismatics, the ubiquity of megachurches, the way we worship, and a broad and increasing ecumenism. American Christianity has changed in perceptible ways, and is sure to keep on changing.[38]

It is inaccurate to say America is not a Christian nation. We have more self-declared Christians than any nation in the world, and our leaders are decidedly Christian. Indeed in 2017 the American Congress was 91 percent Christian, a number that has hardly changed over the last couple of generations.[39] If America doesn't qualify as a Christian nation, then it would be hard to find one that does.

San Antonio, a Return Pilgrimage

In November 2016 I had to attend a conference in San Antonio, Texas. My wife is from the Lone Star State and has family there, so we decided to make a big trip of it, bringing all four of our children with us. San Antonio is a wonderful city with lots to do. And the Mexican food is to die for! But the moment I found out we were headed there, I knew I had to

---

38. For this list I have drawn from Philip Jenkins, "Forty Years On: American Megatrends," *Anxious Bench*, 6 January 2017, located at http://www.patheos.com/blogs/anxiousbench/2017/01/forty-years-on/.

39. Jonah Engel Bromwich, "The New Congress Is 91% Christian. That's Barely Budged Since 1961," *New York Times*, 3 January 2017, located at https://www.nytimes.com/2017/01/03/us/politics/congress-religion-christians.html.

return to Oak Hills Church and see what Max Lucado was up to since the last time I visited—it had been twenty-two years.

Things had changed dramatically from my previous visit two decades prior. In 1994 there were hundreds of worshipers. But in 2016 the attendance was easily in the thousands. My family and I entered in the back and immediately sensed a celebratory feeling in the air as an amazing band played praise music, a choir sang onstage, and video screens all around the auditorium showed the lyrics so we could follow along. We actually struggled to find seating because the indoor arena was so crowded.

Our visit occurred during only one of the four weekend services at the campus. It was packed with people, and was exhilarating. My wife and I both were in tears, not out of sadness, but gladness. We both felt that Lucado's message was perfect for us, and we believe God brought us to that church on that day.

It was like hearing an old friend when Max took the stage. He described all of the service projects the church was doing, various midweek Bible studies, small-group gatherings, children's programs, and other ministries happening. That church is booming and is very much alive.

Oak Hills Church is expanding. They currently have five different locations in San Antonio, one in a nearby city, and another in Brazil—where Max served as a missionary in the 1980s. Their mission statement is "We are the Body of Christ called to be Jesus in every neighborhood in our city and beyond."[40] There is no telling how far this ministry will go.

Oak Hills Church is one of thousands of churches in this nation that continue to inspire, encourage, and serve the needs of the people around them. In every city and every town across the United States similar stories are playing out. Christians come together to heal, to praise God, to work for others, and to be a light in their communities. Addictions are broken, relationships are mended, and hearts are melted. People's lives are changed when they commit to walk in the way of Jesus. That's why the faith continues to proliferate in America and beyond.

Christianity is rising in America. We are in the midst of a national revival.

40. See the church website: http://oakhillschurch.com/beliefs/.

4

The Jesuits: The Greatest Missionaries of All Time . . . and Why They Matter

Perhaps the most famous relic in the world is the Shroud of Turin, located in Italy. This shroud is supposedly the burial cloth used to cover Jesus when he was in the tomb between his crucifixion and death on Good Friday and the resurrection. It is a large strip of linen, around fourteen by four feet. Amazingly, it bears the image of a man that seems to have a beard, long hair, and blood stains on his forehead, hands, and feet. Some scholars claim it is a medieval forgery, while others say that if indeed it was forged, then it was masterfully done, and at a time when tools were far cruder than they are today. Experts have analyzed and debated it for centuries, with different opinions on its authenticity. One thing is clear, however: it has a powerful ability to evoke deep emotions in the Christian.

In 2010 I took a pilgrimage to Turin to see the shroud for myself. It is rarely put on display, but Pope Benedict allowed it that year in order to encourage the faithful through what he called "this holy and extraordinary Icon."[1] I had to book a ticket just to have the chance to enter the church and catch a glimpse of it. After all, the Catholic Church is over a billion members strong, and people from all over the world traveled there to see it.

When I walked into the church—the Cathedral of Saint John the Baptist—I could tell I was in a very sacred setting. Everything was subdued, and all was dark except for the shroud up at the front, which had muted, soft lights behind it to reveal the body of a man. Slowly moving toward the icon, I began to be moved in my soul. Was that the blood of Christ? My entire life I had sung songs about the power of Jesus's blood, and how it washes away the sins of the world.

And that is when I had a strange, profound experience. I looked at a boy in front of me; he was around seven or eight. His face was intense yet innocent. He was looking upward, at the face of his young mother. She was weeping. My heart was deeply moved by the sight of this precious boy, watching his mother venerate the shroud and quietly have a moment with Jesus Christ. He gently touched her hand. It was a loving and holy moment that I will never forget. I do not know what the woman was thinking, but something important was going on inside of her. Was she asking for forgiveness? Was

1. See the pontiff's sermon inspired by his visit to the Turin Shroud in 2010, located at http://w2.vatican.va/content/benedict-xvi/en/speeches/2010/may/documents/hf_ben-xvi_spe_20100502_meditazione-torino.html.

she remembering a deceased friend? Was she suffering from an illness? I wish I knew her thoughts, but of course they will, and deserve to, remain private.

I was so impacted by my experience in front of the shroud that day that I went outside the church into a row of temporary chapels set up for pilgrims, with a priest sitting inside each one to serve the needs of the faithful. I went into a little room labeled "English" and struck up a friendly conversation with an elderly priest who had lived in Quebec when he was younger, and spoke many languages, of which English was one. He was kind and pastoral. He realized the importance of the shroud, and was present to offer spiritual encouragement to those who had received a special grace through the experience.

I have spent my adult life researching and writing about Christianity, and thus the Roman Catholic Church has become a major part of my life and work. I know its history. I lecture on it virtually every day. Every time I sit down to write about church history I surround myself with books that unpack the history of this mammoth institution. With well over a billion baptized members, the Roman Catholic Church is the largest religious organization in the world. The only *human* institutions that rival its size are the nations of China or India.

As a student of the Roman Catholic Church, I fully realize how much I am indebted to it. However, as a Protestant, I have some ambivalence about its history. On the one hand, it is full of examples of how *not* to live the Christian life. On the other hand, there are stories—beautiful stories—of true faith and tenacious commitment to Jesus Christ as Lord: think of St. Francis or St. Clare of Assisi, or Dorothy Day, or Mother Theresa. These are some of the most exemplary Christians in history. Far from perfect, but truly inspiring. Very few of us have the capability or even the desire to live a life so fully committed to the gospel as they were.

The Catholicity of Catholicism

A most impressive aspect of the Roman Catholic Church is its worldwide presence. There are fifteen nations in the world that have a Catholic population of over 20 million members:[2]

Brazil: 165 million

Mexico: 100 million

Philippines: 79 million

United States: 71 million

Italy: 58 million

France: 48 million

Spain: 43 million

Colombia: 43 million

---

2. Catholic statistics come from "Roman Catholic Statistical Update," *International Bulletin of Missionary Research* 38, no. 1 (January 2014): 41–42.

D. R. Congo: 39 million

Argentina: 38 million

Poland: 37 million

Peru: 27 million

Venezuela: 26 million

Germany: 25 million

Nigeria: 25 million

Around 17 percent of the world population is Roman Catholic. And unlike some Protestant denominations, the Roman Catholic Church is growing every year because of its prominence in the global south—where birth rates are comparatively high.

Africa's Catholic population is growing magnificently, faster than anywhere else in the world. It's a similar story in Asia as China now has over nine million Catholics.[3] South Korea—once a Protestant stronghold—has undergone a Catholic boom in recent years. Around 11 percent of South Koreans are now Catholic, and that percentage is growing "across all age groups, among men and women and across all education levels." Pope Francis enjoys extremely high approval ratings in the nation—nearly 90 percent. In

3. See the Pew Research report located here: http://www.pewforum.org/files/2011/12/ChristianityAppendixC.pdf.

comparison, only about 66 percent of Americans hold a favorable view of the pontiff.[4]

Latin America is the most Roman Catholic place in the world. The two largest Catholic nations are Brazil and Mexico, with a combined total of over 250 million members. Latin America and the Caribbean are home to 40 percent of the world's Catholics. Put another way, there are nearly half a billion members of the Roman Catholic Church south of the Rio Grande.

The word "catholic" actually means universal, global, or all-embracing. That word perfectly describes the Roman church. Wherever one travels in the world, there is a good possibility that the Catholic Church is already there, holding mass, conducting ministry, evangelizing, and serving the local population in the name of Christ. And as we will see shortly, one of the biggest reasons for this grand catholicity rests squarely on the shoulders of the Jesuits and their herculean missionary work to the most far-flung places on earth.

In 2011–2012, my family and I lived in Buenos Aires, Argentina, a very Catholic city. We admired the impressive churches and came to appreciate the somewhat private approach to faith there. The churches are open virtually all of the time, and when you pop into one during a weekday afternoon you might find a woman praying quietly in a side chapel. Or perhaps you will see a man sitting on the front row

---

4. Quotation is from Phillip Connor, "6 facts about South Korea's growing Christian population," *Pew Research Center*, 12 August 2014, located at http://www.pewresearch.org/fact-tank/2014/08/12/6-facts-about-christianity-in-south-korea. See also the 2014 Catholic statistics for Korea, located at the website for the Catholic Bishops' Conference of Korea: http://english.cbck.or.kr/news/17070.

staring at the Virgin Mary with tears in his eyes. The Catholic Church is a part of Argentine society in a way Americans do not understand because of our profound religious diversity. Catholicism, however, is the religion of the vast majority of Argentines, and it unites them in tender and admirable ways. There is a sense of community, even among strangers, because of their shared religious heritage.

Little did I know, but a year after we left Argentina the next pope would be elected out of Buenos Aires—Pope Francis.

The election of Pope Francis in 2013 shouldn't have been so surprising. When the previous pope was elected in 2005, insiders reported that it had actually been "something of a horse race" between Joseph Ratzinger and Jorge Bergoglio.[5] As we now know, Ratzinger was elected and became Pope Benedict XVI, only to resign eight years later—something that had not been done by a pope since the year 1415.

When the College of Cardinals met in March 2013, Bergoglio was still considered a viable candidate for the papacy. He was duly elected nonetheless, and took the name Francis, in honor of the great saint of Assisi.

And while the *election* of Pope Francis was not so surprising, there were still a few things about this man that caught the Catholic world off-guard. First of all, and most obviously, he was relatively old to assume the papacy, a position that places tremendous demands on a person's health. Second, he

---

5. John Allen Jr., "Profile: New pope, Jesuit Bergoglio, was runner-up in 2005 conclave," *National Catholic Reporter*, 3 March 2013, located at https://www.ncronline.org/blogs/ncr-today/papabile-day-men-who-could-be-pope-13.

was from Argentina, and the church had never had a Latin American pope before. Third, he was a Jesuit. Before Pope Francis, a Jesuit had never served as pope, a somewhat surprising fact since they are the largest male Catholic order in the world.

Who Are the Jesuits?

Formally, the Jesuits are known as the Society of Jesus (abbreviated as S.J.). They were founded in Paris in the 1530s by a group of seven young men, including an injured Basque soldier named Ignatius Loyola, along with the man who would become arguably the greatest missionary of all time: Francis Xavier. The group was officially approved by the papacy in the year 1540 and promptly began their missionary labors that same year.

The early years of the Jesuits make for a fascinating and inspiring story. Ignatius was a zealous knight with a soft spot for the things of this world: gambling, womanizing, and carousing. More than anything he loved the prestige that came with being a knight, so that he could "live out his fantasies and earn the acclaim deserved by every great knight."[6] He developed a reputation for being a violent man both on and off the battlefield. However, in 1521 a cannonball to the legs cut short his fighting career and nearly killed him.

During his convalescence Ignatius turned to reading the lives of the saints as well as a devotional text called *The*

6. Carlos Eire, *Reformations* (New Haven: Yale University Press, 2016), 443.

Life of Christ, and in short order he became a completely changed man.[7] As soon as he was able to walk he set out on pilgrimage, determined to visit Jerusalem—the holy city. Along the way he stopped in Montserrat, Spain, at the famous Benedictine monastery, and had an intensely religious experience. From there he walked to the town of Manresa and decided to stay, devoting himself to repentance, prayer, and frequent receiving of the mass. He lived in Manresa for about a year—often staying in a cave—developing his influential approach to Christian devotion that was later published as *Spiritual Exercises.* Today, that text is considered one of the great classics of Christian spirituality. In 1523 he fulfilled his vow to visit Jerusalem.

Upon his return to Spain, Ignatius entered into a long period of academic preparation at several Spanish universities. This was during the time of the Inquisition, however, and he continually ran afoul of the church authorities for his novel approach to spirituality—and without a proper license. On multiple occasions they threw him into prison, so he eventually decided to relocate to Paris. It was at the University of Paris that Ignatius acquired a small group of followers, and they all promised to serve the Lord Jesus Christ and "to help souls"—a defining commitment that became their collective vow. Ignatius, Xavier, and company called themselves the Society of Jesus and were all ordained as priests.

Once approved by the pope in 1540, they established a

---

7. *The Life of Christ* was written by Ludolph of Saxony and had only recently been translated into Spanish. It was essentially a manual for prayer, meditation, and private devotions.

home base in Rome. Together they agreed that Ignatius should serve as their superior general for life, and he developed a "semi-military" character for the new organization.[8] However, their true commitment was to the pope, and the Jesuits developed a reputation for absolute submission to his decisions. They committed themselves to outright obedience: "What I see as white, I will believe to be black if the hierarchical Church thus determines it."[9]

Jesuits took the three classical vows for monastics—poverty, chastity, and obedience—but it was their submission to the Roman papacy that set them apart. Their founding document states that they are to completely deny their own will so that they can:

> Do anything that the present Roman pontiff and his successors commands us to do concerning the good of souls and the propagation of the faith . . . in whatever country that he may send us.[10]

Right there in the founding documents they pledged to evangelize the Muslim world (the "Turks"), travel to the remotest corners of the world, enter into the nations under Protestant control, and minister to the faithful wherever they may be.

The Bishop of Rome must have been pleased, for indeed he made use of these young men who threw themselves at his

---

8. Jacques Blocher and Jacques Blandenier, *The Evangelization of the World*, trans. Michael Parker (Pasadena, CA: William Carey Library, 2013), 141.

9. George Ganss, ed., *Spiritual Exercises*, in *Ignatius of Loyola: Spiritual Exercises and Selected Works* (New York: Paulist, 1991), 211–14.

10. See Blocher and Blandenier, *The Evangelization of the World*, 142.

feet. Pope after pope sent the Jesuits out to traverse the entire known and unknown world. This all occurred at a time—the first time in history—that one group of people actually had the capacity to circumnavigate the earth. The Europeans with their newfound marine technology set out to discover new lands, gain possessions for their crown, and claim millions of souls for Christ. It was the Jesuits who were called, explicitly, to take on the great task of evangelization. And history shows us that they were remarkably successful in their work.

The Jesuit Difference

The Jesuits were not just another monastic order. Their whole approach was different, and it wasn't just because of their resolute fealty to the papacy. They were untypical in virtually every way: no official garb, no set times for prayer, and no desire to cloister themselves away from the rest of the world. Rather, the Jesuits were approved by the pope to get things done. First and foremost, they were commissioned to win souls away from the Protestants who were growing fantastically across Europe. The pope needed these holy soldiers to brave the Protestant-Catholic borderlands and figure out ways to stifle the Lutheran advance. As history shows, Luther's revolution essentially split Europe in two: a Protestant north and a Catholic south, but there was so much territory in the middle that was fought for, both through military might as well as through theological and pastoral wars. And the Jesuits, more often than not, won those battles for European hearts and minds.

Jesuits were expected not to aspire to higher office in the church, a fact that helps explain why a Jesuit priest was not chosen to be pope until 2013. Jesuits were to be missionaries, not bishops and cardinals. It was not their job to sit down in some cathedral and push paper, as so many church administrators had to do.

Rather, Jesuits were pioneers, men of adventure, men of the world. "The whole world was their cloister."[11] They weren't even called to live in community. So many Jesuits set out by themselves. They were some of the bravest explorers in history. Instead of guns and bayonets, they equipped themselves with prayer and Scripture. But they functioned with a shield of sorts—papal approval. Popes knew that wherever they sent the Jesuits, the Jesuits would go. Self-sacrifice was balanced with a sense of mission and purpose.

This new style of Christian monasticism was attractive. These men climbed mountains, sailed the open seas, and sacrificed their lives for a cause much greater than themselves. They were flexible and noble, and developed a reputation for impressive courage in the face of danger.

And their numbers grew dramatically. Beginning in 1540 with seven men, they bloomed to 1,000 brothers by the time of Ignatius's death in 1556. By 1566 they had achieved a membership of 3,500. By 1580 they were at 5,000 members. In the year 1615, just a couple of generations after the order's founding, the Jesuits had grown to 13,000 brothers stationed at mission points all over the world.

---

11. Eire, *Reformations*, 451.

Wonderful movies have been made about the global adventures of the Jesuits. Perhaps the most famous is *The Mission* (1986), starring Robert De Niro, Jeremy Irons, Liam Neeson, and Aidan Quinn. This film is astonishing in its cinematography—for which it won an academy award. It is based on true events surrounding the Treaty of Madrid in 1750. Jesuits worked hard to evangelize and protect the Guarani Indian tribe of northern Argentina and Paraguay, only to have their work completely destroyed by Portuguese slave traders. They built up a successful mission above the Iguazu Falls. Initially they were under Spanish protection, which meant slavery was not promoted. But when the treaty was made, the Jesuit missions in the area were ceded to Portugal—a slave-trading nation. War and chaos broke out, and the missions were left in ruins. Only a few children managed to escape with their lives.

Another film about Jesuits is *Black Robe* (1991). It takes place in French Canada, at the time called New France, and tells the story of a remote Jesuit mission to the Huron Indians. It is set in the Beaver Wars of the seventeenth century, where the Iroquois Confederacy, Huron, and Algonquin tribes went to war over the lucrative fur trade. The Europeans paid good money for the animal pelts, so there was much at stake for the warring tribes. The film ends with the Huron acceptance of Roman Catholic Christianity, but explains that only a few years later the Huron were massacred by the Iroquois, and the mission was completely destroyed.

A third Jesuit film, directed by acclaimed director Martin

Scorsese, is *Silence* (2016). Starring Andrew Garfield and Liam Neeson, it deals with a famous Jesuit mission to Japan in the seventeenth century. It is based on the brutal persecution of Catholics in Japan during a period of intense nationalism in the 1630s. It was one of the most successful persecutions of Christians in history in the sense that Christianity was almost wiped out after a century of steady growth. The film plunges deeply into matters of faith and doubt, causing viewers to relate to the Jesuit priests who must make painful choices. If they convert people, then their converts could potentially die. By apostatizing, however, the Japanese could live their lives in peace.

The beauty of these three films is that they show the tremendous complexity of what it must have been like for those Jesuits who went to the remotest corners of the world—Iguazu Falls, French Canada, and Japan—in order to spread the gospel of Christ. Where these films fall short, however, is in their portrayal of Jesuit missions as colossal failures. In all three cases, the missions were destroyed and all that the Jesuits had built came to nothing. In reality, these three films portray exceptions, not the rule.

The truth is that the Jesuits experienced success on a scale that Christianity had scarcely experienced before, and has rarely experienced since. They changed the religious demography of the world during their most fruitful centuries, from about 1540 to their suppression in the late 1700s. The Jesuits became so influential that they were expelled for a period of time, only to be restored in 1814. For about two and a half centuries, however, the Jesuits planted the Christian faith in some of the most remarkably complex and remote places. All Christians everywhere should be grateful for their service.

Saint Francis Xavier: The Greatest Missionary

When it comes to missionaries, one is hard-pressed to find someone greater than St. Francis Xavier (1506–1552). Perhaps the only missionary who accomplished more is the apostle Paul. In fact, Xavier and the great apostle have a lot in common. Neither of them settled for very long when they were in the missionary field. Their peripatetic careers were not in vain, however, as they both seemed to prefer life on the move, in an effort to discover new people and places in need of Christ.

Francis Xavier was a Spaniard. He moved to Paris at the age of nineteen to study philosophy. While there, he began worshiping with a group of Protestants and nearly converted. However, he was soon befriended by a much older student named Ignatius Loyola, who eventually made quite an impression on him.[12] At first, Xavier thought Ignatius was a bit too religious for his tastes, "excessively austere and pious."[13] Xavier was only twenty-three and Ignatius was thirty-eight. However, Francis was struggling financially, and Ignatius was a man of means. They became roommates and began to recruit others into their little band of brothers

---

12. Paul Spickard and Kevin Cragg, *A Global History of Christians* (Grand Rapids, MI: Baker, 1994), 208.
13. Blocher and Blandenier, *The Evangelization of the World*, 177.

that started calling themselves the Society of Jesus, later known as the Jesuits.

In 1541 the king of Portugal asked Ignatius Loyola for four missionaries to go to Goa, India—the famous Portuguese bridgehead to Asia. Ignatius said he could spare only two of his men, but they coaxed him to allow three. The day before they set out, one of the men became sick and was replaced by Xavier. The great missionary to Asia was given one day to prepare for a journey that took him far away from Europe for the rest of his life.[14] His long sea voyage to India began on 7 April 1541, which happened to be his thirty-fifth birthday. For a solid decade Xavier threw himself completely into missionary work, until his death off the coast of China in 1552.

Due to sea turbulence, Xavier's ship anchored and wintered at Portuguese Mozambique off the southeastern coast of Africa for eight months. During March 1542 they made their way to India, and landed at Goa on 6 May 1542, a full thirteen months after their departure.

Goa is on the west coast of India and was the capital of Portuguese India from 1510 to 1961. Shortly after their arrival, Xavier was appointed as the director of St. Paul's College—an appointment that proved hugely significant in missions history. From Xavier's time on, Jesuits have been associated with offering excellent education in the mission field, an issue we will address shortly.

Xavier's tenure in the college did not last long because he wanted to evangelize. Within months of his arrival in India,

---

14. Spickard and Cragg, *A Global History of Christians*, 208.

he set off again, this time to the other side of India where he could evangelize the Paravar—a fisher caste on the southeast coast, right across the gulf from Sri Lanka. He evangelized the Paravars for about three years, establishing dozens of churches in the region, despite the fact that he could not speak their language. He kept his focus on the lower castes, a strategy that proved to be brilliant. He also focused intensely on evangelizing children, with the hopes that they would teach the gospel to their parents, a counterintuitive approach that in this case worked marvelously.

In 1545 Xavier set sail again. He stopped to evangelize in Ceylon (now Sri Lanka), and then moved on to Malacca (now Malaysia) and later to the Moluccas—known at the time as the Spice Islands (in modern-day Indonesia). He evangelized Malaysia and Indonesia for around three years, planting churches, looking after the sick, and catechizing children —which proved to be one of his greatest gifts.

After a quick trip back to Goa, Xavier sailed for Japan in 1549, becoming one of the first Europeans to set foot there. He had sudden and impressive success in his missionary labors. At the age of forty-three he was seemingly at his best. His strategy in Japan shifted, however, as he tried to reach out to the upper classes.

Xavier was extremely impressed by the Japanese. He thought they were courteous, literate, and sophisticated. He tried to learn the Japanese language and culture, with moderate success. Xavier made around two thousand converts in Japan and established five Christian communities. More importantly, he planted seeds that produced a bountiful harvest. In only fifty years after his departure, the church in Japan grew to 300,000 members. Had the great persecution of Japanese Christians in the 1630s never happened, Japan would have become one of the great centers of Asian Christianity.[15]

In 1552 Xavier returned to Goa for a few months and then set sail for his final journey. He made it all the way to Shangchuan (known to the Portuguese as St. John's), located just off the southeastern coast of China. He forgot his official papers and was denied entry to China's mainland. The journey had been exceedingly difficult this time, and many of those on board became very sick, as did Xavier. He took fever and died rather suddenly, at the age of forty-six.

Xavier was already treated as a saint late in life. His corpse was taken back to Goa where it remains to the present, in a rather well-preserved state. When I took a pilgrimage to his relics in 2014 I saw for myself just how well preserved his body remains. Xavier is deeply revered in Goa, as he is known by the honorific title, "the apostle to the Far East." His right arm—by which he baptized thousands—was severed after his death and taken to Rome where it is still enshrined in the tomb of St. Ignatius Loyola, in the Church of the Gesù.

Xavier's impressive missionary accomplishments were matched by his character. He was respected as a man of true holiness. Although he initially found it off-putting, even-

---

15. For the number of converts in Japan, see Eire, *Reformations*, 500. For the 300,000 members in Japan, see Spickard and Cragg, *A Global History of Christians*, 208.

tually he chose the deeply religious path that his mentor Ignatius of Loyola had taken years before. Xavier was so pious that people attributed miracles to him with regularity. They said he levitated when he administered the Eucharist. He was sought after because of his healing abilities. To the faithful in Goa, his relics still exude power.

Xavier's piety was legendary and his love for Christ was well known to all who met him. He prayed all night sometimes. He was ascetic in his approach to the faith, eating little, fasting often, and putting his body through unbelievable rigors, which may have killed him in the end, in addition to the sheer exhaustion of a life on the seas. The tropical climate of Asia was oppressive and physically taxing. Clean water was scarce and nutritious food in short supply while at sail.

The number of converts made by Xavier will never be fully known. The range is anywhere from tens of thousands to over a million. There can be no doubt, however, that he played a major role in what became a robust and sprawling network of Catholic churches in the Far East, which survive to the present day.

With the lone exception of the apostle Paul, no missionary has captured the imagination of Christians as has Xavier. His many letters give us a glimpse into a man who struggled to learn Asian languages, who spent incalculable time listening to confessions, who had a passion to reach the poor and sick, who invested great time and energy into understanding other cultures, and who stopped at nothing to bring the gospel to as many as possible.[16]

Xavier inspired the Jesuits after him, and served as a bell-wether for how to do missions in distant lands. He became famous during his own lifetime because of his letters, which were being published in different European languages shortly after they reached Europe. Perhaps most importantly, Xavier stirred a fire in the hearts of Jesuits to bring Christianity to the world, no matter how difficult it might be. In his wake, Jesuits fanned out all over Asia, Africa, Latin America, and Oceania in hopes of converting thousands of souls to Christ as the great Xavier did.

But Xavier also instilled in the hearts of the Jesuits a true and sincere Christian faith. During his life he was accredited with miracles due to his deep piety. After his death, he became mythical. For example, the numbers of converts attributed to him grew to the point of absurdity. Some claimed he converted over a million people—a number which, of course, is far too high.[17] Others claimed he had the gift of prophecy. Some even accredited Xavier with resurrecting the dead, a rumor that caused serious misgivings in the church. He was made a saint in the year 1622, and his well-preserved body continues to draw crowds to Goa each year.[18]

The Society of Jesus became prestigious and bore a cachet

16. On his difficulty in learning languages, see Blocher and Blandenier, *The Evangelization of the World*, 185.
17. The Catholic Church grew quickly after Xavier, and it is likely that by the time people learned of Christianity in some of Xavier's mission points, those same churches had grown substantially. Thus it was an error of conflation. People knew that Christianity had grown rapidly, but they did not necessarily know that the lion's share of growth occurred after Xavier's departure from those places.
18. See William Pinch, "The Corpse and Cult of Francis Xavier, 1552–1623," in *Engag-*

closely aligned with the extraordinary life of Francis Xavier. Adventurous men in the prime of life were inspired by Xavier's legendary missionary travels and his eloquent and often exotic missionary reports. Indeed, Xavier's habits of sending detailed letters to the mother church became standard practice. And Jesuits became excellent note-takers when they went into the mission field. They acquired a truly impressive ability to describe the people, the culture, the fauna and flora, and even the local economy.

In many ways the Jesuits were the first field anthropologists, with one major exception: after Xavier, most of them stayed in the places where they were sent. Instead of moving on every few years, as did Xavier, they usually gave their lives to the people they served, often for decades. Suddenly the Western world was having an influence on China, Japan, India, and other places that had little contact with the West prior to the Jesuits.

Quite suddenly, the Jesuits had become the most important order in the Roman Catholic Church, and the other orders became jealous, to the point of shutting down the Jesuits from 1759 to 1814.[19] The Jesuits were viewed with suspicion because they were absolutely committed to the church—and not necessarily to the European powers that were frenetically

---

ing South Asian Religions, ed. Mathew Schmalz and Peter Gottschalk (Albany: State University of New York Press, 2011), 113–32.

19. They were not shut down everywhere all at once. The Portuguese Empire suppressed them in 1759, and various places followed. The Spanish Empire suppressed them in 1767. The papacy (Pope Clement XIV) itself suppressed the order in 1773. They were never formally suppressed, however, in Russia or in the newly established United States.

planting themselves all over the world. In general, the Dominicans and Franciscans believed the Jesuits to be theologically suspect for dressing like the locals, assimilating to their culture, and basically becoming a member of that society for the sake of the gospel. Many in the Catholic Church thought the Jesuits had sold out, watered down the true Catholic faith, and had crossed many lines in the task of evangelization.

Some of the greatest Catholic missionaries in history were Jesuits—and were inspired by the groundbreaking work of Xavier. In South India, Italian Jesuit Robert de Nobili served for fifty years in the first half of the seventeenth century. French Jesuit Alexandre de Rhodes worked in Vietnam around the same time. Alessandro Valignano was an Italian Jesuit who picked up Xavier's work in Japan and had tremendous success before the faith was virtually eradicated through persecution. Italian Jesuit Matteo Ricci made a huge impact on the imperial court of China during his nearly thirty-year ministry that began in 1682. Spanish Jesuit St. Peter Claver worked among the slaves in Colombia, baptizing tens of thousands of people in the seventeenth century. French Jesuit St. Jean de Brébeuf served for twenty years among the Huron in Canada, only to be tortured and martyred by some Iroquois in 1649. Ippolito Desideri (died 1733) was an Italian Jesuit who worked in Tibet and wrote the earliest accurate accounts of this remote region and its people.

What the Jesuits Can Teach Us

The Jesuits were geniuses at spreading the gospel, and they have much to teach Christians of all denominations today. We have to remember, however, that this was a different time, when missionaries went to their destination and stayed for life. For various reasons, this approach is not common today.

But perhaps it should be. The Jesuits can teach us a lesson here. They trained for their mission, and when they arrived they became avid learners. They tried to figure out all aspects of the local culture: language, customs, religion, and political context. Instead of evangelizing first, they listened first. Evangelizing without getting to know the people is premature. However, in the process of understanding other cultures, they assimilated. And this is why many of their peers condemned them. They thought the Jesuits surrendered too much of their own culture when they entered another. Today, many Christians take the Jesuit methods for granted: missionaries should seek first to understand, and then to be understood.

It is remarkable how the Jesuits were drawn to the poor and disenfranchised. They regularly ministered to prisoners, prostitutes, and orphans. Jesuit missions were often accused of sheltering Indians from slavery. They gravitated toward African slave populations in the New World. They worked among the Natives in Canada and America, rather than simply pastoring European communities. Yes, there were many Jesuits—like de Nobili and Ricci—who worked among the highest echelons of Indian and Chinese society, but the majority of Jesuits chose to work in the lower strata. Xavier's career was unique in that he worked both sides of the spectrum at various points of his ministry, always with the goal to win as many as possible.

Finally, we must note that the Jesuits are famous for educating the people they encountered. Beginning from the first decade of the order's existence, their prime strategy was to educate young boys and turn them into good Catholics. Inevitably, they believed, the parents and possibly even the nation would follow.

The Jesuit foray into education began almost accidentally in 1548 when they were asked to open a school for children in Messina, on the island of Sicily. Ignatius Loyola was at first reluctant to get into the business of education since he wanted to focus on missions. However, just months after opening the school, it was clear they had stumbled onto something important. "Requests began to pour in for the establishment of more schools," and they were all funded by wealthy Catholics. Jesuit "colleges" (their preferred term) popped up all over Europe at breakneck speed. In only twenty years they opened 150 educational institutions. By 1606 they had 293 institutions all over the world. That number grew to 370 by the year 1615, and there were 13,000 Jesuits to staff these schools and conduct missions and ministry.[20]

The Jesuit approach to education was both religious and

20. Eire, *Reformations*, 452.

secular in nature. They introduced all manner of disciplines into the curriculum, including grammar, rhetoric, Latin, Greek, Hebrew, pagan literature, geometry, theater, astronomy, botany, theology, philosophy, history, political theory, and various arts such as sculpting. It was a spectacular education for young people, and it was absolutely free. Jesuits were firmly committed to the principle of free education, as inscribed onto the entrance of their earliest (1551) institution in Rome: "School of Grammar, Humanities, and Christian Doctrine, Free."[21]

Free education resulted in many young people coming under the influence of the Roman Catholic Church. Even in Protestant lands the Jesuits made significant gains. Early in the 1500s, the Roman Catholic authorities saw the Jesuits as a potentially helpful tool for stymieing the progress of the Protestant Reformation. No one could have imagined at the time how effective they would become, not only in preventing Catholic losses, but in gaining souls both in Europe and on far distant shores.[22]

The Society of Jesus proved to be a great benefit to the Roman Catholic Church in the decades following the Reformation. To Protestants, the Jesuits were a significant challenge. It took Protestants a century and a half to mobilize effectively, and Protestant missions did not even launch until the early 1700s. By that time, it was clear that the Roman

---

21. Eire, *Reformations*, 452.
22. For how Jesuits outmaneuvered Protestants, see Diarmaid MacCulloch, *Christianity: The First Three Thousand Years* (London: Penguin, 2011), 666–78, 706.

Catholics had outmaneuvered them and had planted themselves all over the face of the earth.

Today, however, we are in an ecumenical era. Catholics and Protestants serve shoulder to shoulder in the task of global evangelism. To be sure, there are disagreements, most fundamentally over the authority of the Roman bishop. But overall, the advance of Christianity, whether in its Protestant, Orthodox, or Catholic guise, is applauded by all who profess the name of Jesus. The global church has matured a great deal in this regard. And let us hope that this ecumenical sensibility continues to flourish.

Here is an amazing statistic: of the 376 Jesuits who set out for China between 1581 and 1712, fully 127 of them died at sea on the way to their destination.[23] All Christians should take inspiration from the Jesuits, their charity work, their innovations in education, and their courageous mission work. These men gave their lives that Christianity might rise up one day.

And Christianity is rising. Those who travel internationally see this process unfolding globally. Without the pioneering efforts of the Jesuits, this growth would not be nearly as vibrant as it currently is.

The story of the Jesuit missionaries needs to be revisited and retold so that we—both Protestant and Catholic—can be inspired by them. I am amazed at the deep faith they cultivated in themselves as well as in the hearts of the people they served. Surveying two millennia of Christian faith, the Jesuits

23. Diarmaid MacCulloch, *The Reformation* (New York: Penguin, 2003), 440.

are rather unique in the way they gave their lives to Christ. And by doing so they transformed civilizations.

In the year 1996, Mary Doria Russell published a futuristic novel called *The Sparrow*. It tells the story of a newly discovered planet called Rakhat and a Jesuit mission to take the gospel to the inhabitants of the planet. Of course, as in the Hollywood renditions, everything falls apart, virtually everyone dies, and in the end we are left pondering whether Christian evangelization was a huge mistake.

If that was the end of the story, however, we would not be talking about Christianity being the largest religion in the world, and how it continues to rise in unexpected places. Indeed, Christianity has gone global, and it is by far the most widespread religion in human history. And the Jesuit missions contributed profoundly to its expansion. Marginalized people were given dignity. People with little access to education received it, for free. Prostitutes, orphans, prisoners, and other rejected people were given their dignity back. People of low caste and low repute were brought into the Christian fold, and thrived.

Today, when we visit places like Nigeria, Brazil, or the Philippines, and see the beauty of the gospel being lived out, we can only give thanks for people like the Jesuits, people who died to themselves that Christ may rise. I am reminded of John the Baptist's joyful exultation upon realizing that Jesus was the promised messiah: "He must increase, but I must decrease" (John 3:30).

The Jesuits lived that proclamation as if it was their own.

5

African Encounters with Christianity

Dear Rev. Prof. Dyron:

It was not me who saved your life. Our good Lord God used me to save your life. I didn't know you but God brought you into my life. Why? He knows why. You didn't know, but the man had big plans to beat and rob you. When he was at the reception in my office one of my secretaries heard him calling the other men, telling them that you are in my office, so they were told to wait at the gate on your way to the university. The man had bad intentions of stealing your things, or to do something bad to you.

—The Very Rev. Enos Omodhi, Uhuru Highway Lutheran Cathedral

It was the summer of 2010. It was my first time to Africa, and during the trip I was swiftly introduced to the good, the bad, and the ugly.

The Good, the Bad, and the Ugly

First, the good. I attended a conference at the Nairobi Evangelical Graduate School of Theology, where our topic was Politics, Poverty, and Prayer. We enjoyed a wonderful gathering with a rich array of papers, presentations, and opportunities for fellowship. One of the things that first struck me was how different East Africans are from West Africans. The majority of the conference attendees were from the East—mainly Kenya, Tanzania, and Uganda. However, during the conference, I shared a guesthouse with Nigerians. The East Africans seemed more laid-back, with softer personalities, and a bit more approachable. The Nigerians were extremely friendly, but more forceful. Every one of them struck me as being quite ambitious, outgoing, and entrepreneurial. Not unlike North America, people in different regions of Africa have different characteristics.

I'll never forget the distinguished speaker from Uganda—a hierarch in the Anglican Communion—who flatly told us that Islam would eventually eclipse Christianity in his country because Muslims are far more unified. I found this a bit surprising because Uganda is a strongly Christian nation, around 85 percent. However, after the conference I realized that he was onto something. Over the last twenty-five years or so, Islam's growth in Uganda has been around 2 percent per decade, whereas Christianity is losing members each year, albeit slightly. In addition, Muslims almost always have higher fertility rates than Christians because they usually prohibit contraceptives. The speaker's lesson was memorable because he pulled no punches. The audience was almost entirely Christian, but he unabashedly delivered the news that Christianity was not as healthy in certain parts of Africa as we might want to believe.

One of the most important lessons I learned about African Christianity at that 2010 conference is that Africans tend to be mission-minded. They don't keep Christianity to themselves and are, therefore, transforming their continent. Whether by addressing underlying issues of poverty, or working to overcome the short life expectancy, or trying to combat violence, they are full of hope for the future.

In recent years there has been much discussion about reverse-missions, the phenomenon of Christians from the global south missionizing the Western world—the place that sent missionaries to them in years past. Reverse missions are usually associated with Korean Christians because of their tremendous resolve to send missionaries all over the world. But in Nairobi I saw that Africans are equally as zealous to spread the gospel, and they are particularly eager to plant the gospel in Europe—where in some cases Christianity is on life-support. Already the United States and Europe are home to thousands of churches started by Africans; for example, the Nigerian-based Redeemed Christian Church of God has already planted hundreds of churches in the U.S. and has built a $15-million Redemption Camp in Floyd, Texas.[1]

During one of the conference tea breaks I overheard two African clergymen discussing their plans to take the gospel to the indigenous peoples. At first thought, I figured they were talking about remote villages in Africa. But when I listened further, I realized they were talking about the citizens of Great Britain. I had heard about reverse missions for years, but it was really fascinating to hear Africans actually making plans to bring the gospel back to the people who had brought it to them. I had to smile. How ironic that only a hundred years ago British missionaries were having those very same conversations. But a century later, the tables have turned. Now, instead of the British evangelizing the natives of Africa, it is the Africans who are evangelizing the natives of Great Britain.

Second, the bad. In virtually all of the continent's countries, Africans struggle mightily just to survive. Famine in South Sudan. Massacres in the Democratic Republic of Congo. Terrorism and kidnappings in Nigeria. Violent persecution against Christians in Egypt. Dictatorships in Zimbabwe, Angola, Sudan, Swaziland, and elsewhere. Rampant poverty. Lack of educational opportunities. By far the shortest life expectancy in the world.

I had never seen so many unemployed men standing around as I did when I went to Africa for the first time. With

1. See Jerome Socolovsky, "Nigerian Church Has Huge Expansion Plans in US," *Voice of America*, 25 October 2013, located at https://www.voanews.com/a/nigerian-church-has-huge-expansion-plans-in-us/1777453.html.

so many young men out of work, desperate to start a family and have some dignity, but with no money to enable them, they turn to crime. In many African contexts there is simply no hope because there are so few jobs. For the millions who have little formal education, it is truly a dismal future. It is no understatement to say that, economically, much of Africa is in crisis. One visit to Africa—almost anywhere on the continent—reveals socioeconomic problems that dwarf what we are used to in the Western world.

Third, the ugly. This is where the letter at the beginning of this chapter comes into play.

My conference was not really in Nairobi per se. It was actually several miles outside the city on the beautiful and idyllic campus of Africa International University. Mornings are quiet on the compound. Everyone is either already highly educated, or working on their education. People eat their meals in peace, and there is plenty of food. I accidentally left my laptop in a building one day and returned a long time later; it was still sitting where I left it. That wouldn't have happened in the city.

At the end of the conference I made a trip to the heart of downtown—to River Road. I booked a rather cheap hotel located near to the University of Nairobi, where I had to do some research for a few days. When I told the driver at the conference where I needed to go, he was confused. "You're staying on River Road? Are you sure?" I later found out that River Road had a reputation, and it wasn't good. It was crime infested and known for prostitutes. I have traveled a lot, however, and have learned that Westerners are usually too easily frightened. Seasoned travelers know how to conduct themselves in these kinds of places, and rarely does anything bad happen.

My hotel seemed nice enough, but I found out there were problems inside. On just the first day there I met a fellow American who suspected that his laptop was stolen from his hotel room by one of the employees, and he claimed to know who it was. The next day he actually paid that employee some bribe money, and miraculously the computer reappeared while he was out.

Without going into detail, I can confirm that River Road has prostitutes. And they are patronized by men—including Western men—in the hotel where I stayed.

During the few days I was on River Road I learned of a double homicide not far from my hotel. I quickly realized that whenever I left my room I should probably make a beeline to the university rather than wandering around in the area. However, that's precisely where I made my mistake.

The day before I left Kenya, I decided to get my courage up and explore. So I did. And I happened to be checking out the Holy Family Catholic Cathedral when I was approached by a friendly young man around the age of twenty. We hit it off, and were enjoying a nice chat while we walked around the area. I felt rather safe with a local person at my side. So I let my guard down and before long we had covered some good ground. However, I realized that we were virtually alone on a side street. And that's when two other men approached me, asking for money. I turned to the guy with me and he said he would take care of me if I would just stick close to him. The other two guys kept harassing me, however. They weren't physically touching me, but each time they approached me they inched closer. They wanted something from me. They were not speaking English (although I presumed they could), but were speaking to each other in their own tongue, probably Swahili.

I was uncomfortable. Rarely do I panic in my travels, but this time I did. In the distance I noticed a towering cross that appeared to be connected to a church building. Realizing I had made a costly error, I made a quick calculation and burst off running as fast as I could. While running I turned my head only to realize they were chasing me. I can run fairly fast, but I had no idea where I was headed. Was it a church? Or was it just a cross? If it was a church, then would it be open? In Africa there are often fences around properties.

After running for probably ten minutes I arrived at the church and, yes, it was surrounded by a walled fence. However, realizing I was in need, the security guard let me in. I went into the church and requested to see the pastor. The young man who had befriended me came in behind me, saying he was with me. Finally the secretary told me I would be allowed into the office area in order to meet with the pastor. Once I encountered the pastor I realized I was safe, and I was incredibly thankful.

I explained my situation to the pastor and he said it was common for robbers to work in groups. I told him about the man I had befriended, who was in the waiting room. The pastor told me to rest easy; he said he would take care of me, and would even drive me directly to my hotel after some time. After I calmed down he told me to follow him to the parking lot, but on the way out I came face to face with the young man who had followed me, and he said, "Would you please come outside and talk with me privately for a minute?" Stupidly, I said yes. So we walked outside and he asked me, point blank, for money. He said, "I saved you from those two robbers, so you need to give me some cash for that." I obliged and gave him a handful of shillings—what was probably no more than twenty dollars. He wanted more, but by now the pastor was making his way toward us.

The pastor took me to my hotel, and later that day he emailed me the letter at the beginning of this chapter. Without being overly dramatic, I think things could have gone very differently that day. That's certainly what the pastor thought. I'll never know what might have occurred had I not made the decision to sprint toward that cross.

That night I contacted my parents and my wife to let them know of the close call. I probably should have waited until I returned to the U.S. because I still had to spend a couple of weeks in Ethiopia. I hate for my family to worry about me when I travel. But in this case I truly felt like I had dodged a bullet—maybe literally. And I felt they needed to know.

The next morning I hailed a cab and made my way to the airport. I asked the driver to take me to a currency exchange business not far from the airport. My head was still spinning.

I handed over a large wad of around 20,000 shillings (about $200 USD) to the employee and told her I needed American dollars in return. She gave me just under 100 dollars. I told her she only gave me half of what I expected. She said, "Sir, you only gave me 10,000 shillings." I had been fooled.

I had broken the first rule of currency exchange. Always count your money out loud. Never hand over cash without first agreeing to how much cash you are handing over. I had counted my blessings since escaping the threesome on the streets of Nairobi, only to get nailed by a friendly cashier at what seemed like a bona fide establishment.

It was ugly. But you live and learn. A mere 100 dollars is nothing compared to what might have gone wrong on that trip.

This story is a microcosm of Africa: deep pressures, but beautiful examples of true faith. One sees desperately poor people, but also those who are rich in faith and hospitality. There is hope in many places, but despair in even more. In Africa one finds enclaves of literacy, civility, and virtue—like the campus where I stayed in Nairobi. But there are also plenty of areas that are dangerous, unsuitable for business or tourism, and certainly not a place for foreigners to wander around.

Recently I read about one woman's courageous efforts to make a difference in Nairobi. Levina Musumba Mulandi believes that discipleship is the way to move fellow women "past survival mode and onto the highway of economic empowerment, spiritual wholeness, and emotional wellness."

She calls herself a disciple maker and believes that, with the power of Christ, God will bring healing and restoration to "ruined and devastated cities" like Nairobi, one life at a time (Isaiah 61:1–4).

Mulandi's life is representative of many women in Africa: she was "at-risk . . . struggling to survive." And that's when an older woman came to her rescue and discipled her, showing her how to move forward. For most African women, qualifying for a university is a mere fantasy. However, with a comprehensive strategy that can only be attained by the help of a mentor, it is possible. With her husband, Mulandi now pastors the 2000-member Nairobi Baptist Church, and she mentors women in her home country of Kenya, as well as other women in Tanzania, Uganda, and Rwanda. She also lectures at Nairobi's International Leadership University.[2]

A Story of Hope

Despite instability, widespread corruption, and even the most basic of human problems such as famine, I choose to believe that Africa's future is bright. As anyone who has done a mission trip to Africa can testify, there is extraordinary faith there. Africans rely on God to an extent that Westerners don't really have to. In the West we have first-world problems: which university we should attend, how deeply we should engage social media, and whether or not we should take a

2. Levina Musumba Mulandi, "How Discipleship Is Transforming Nairobi, One Woman at a Time," *Christianity Today*, June 2017, located at http://www.christianitytoday.com/women/2017/june/discipleship-transforming-nairobi-one-woman-at-time.html.

gap year before or after college. Africa's problems are of an entirely different order. And those African Christians who rely on their faith in Christ inevitably become strong in the faith, causing me to wonder why more Africans don't come to the West to do missions to us, rather than us thinking we have so much to offer them.

In truth, Africans *are* bringing their faith to the West, through immigration. Especially in Europe, we see Africans establishing churches in some of the most ardently secular places. For instance, in London, it looks like the future of Christianity there is in the hands of Africans who are establishing Pentecostal churches all over the city. In 2016 *Christianity Today* reported, "For every Anglican church that closed in London since 2010, more than three Pentecostal churches opened."[3] And some of them are large, especially considering the city's long slide into secularization. For instance, the Kingsway International Christian Centre in northeast London ministers to 12,000 members and has planted churches in many other countries.[4]

However encouraging, the stories of African migrants who succeed in the West pale in comparison to the intense poverty faced by so many in Africa. And while development continues to progress in Africa, Christians must challenge the notion that increased wealth is what really matters in this life.

3. "Jesus is alive in London," *Christianity Today*, May 2016, p. 15, no author mentioned.
4. For 12,000 members, see the website of the church's pastor, Matthew Ashimolowo, located at http://www.pastormatthew.tv/index.php/2014-01-23-08-36-52/about-us. For international branches of Kingsway, see the church website at https://www.kicc.org.uk/branches/#1439920057809-792c554b-4990.

In the gospels, Jesus frequently contrasts the rich and the poor. And more often than not it is the rich who get chastised, and the poor who come across as exemplary. For example, his beatitudes evince a preferential option for poor people. He seems to take their side, for example when he pronounces that the last shall be first and the first shall be last (Matthew 19:30), as well as the idea that those who are rich have already received their reward here on earth (Luke 6:24). Other examples permeate the gospels:

- When Jesus first launched his ministry, he quoted Isaiah 61:1, "The Spirit of the Lord God is upon me, because the Lord has anointed me to bring good news to the poor" (Luke 4:18).

- In the Parable of the Sheep and the Goats (Matthew 25) Jesus links salvation to taking care of the have-nots, in spite of the fact that there will always be poor people in our midst (Mark 14:7).

- Jesus warns that anyone who cannot give up their possessions cannot be his disciple (Luke 14:33).

- While it would be misguided to think Jesus absolutely opposed worldly wealth, his critiques could be stinging. He explodes in anger at the moneychangers in the temple (Matthew 21:12–13). He criticizes the Pharisees for their love of money (Luke 16:14–15), and even makes the point that it is extraordinarily difficult for a rich person to enter the kingdom of God (Matthew 19:23–26).

- In the Sermon on the Mount, Jesus commands his disciples not to lay up treasures on earth because ". . . where your treasure is, there your heart will be also" (Matthew 6:19).

Theologically, increased wealth is not necessarily a blessing. According to the teachings of Jesus, it is more like a curse. It is difficult for a rich person to sell everything and give to the poor. It is much easier to follow Jesus when one has so little to begin with.

While African Christians often struggle to make ends meet, their faith is powerful and inspiring. And it matches well with what Jesus is getting at in the gospels. Many Westerners read the gospels from a certain distance due to our relative economic security. Most Africans, however, can clearly understand Jesus's references to the poor and marginalized. They read those texts and see *themselves*. There are striking parallels between the biblical and African contexts.

In a spiritual sense, we could say Africans—living on the poorest continent—are the haves and we in the West are the have-nots. We can certainly bring medicine, education, and earthly opportunities into the lives of Africans, but Africans are well positioned to breathe new life into our souls. They may benefit from our benevolent efforts, but we also stand in need of them, their faith, and their profound reliance on Christ in a world so full of hardship.

I think a promising model for Christian missions would be for American churches to sponsor a group of Africans to come here rather than us going there. Struggling or dying churches would benefit tremendously by hosting on-fire

African Christians into their congregations for, say, a summer. I would make the problems of Africa more vivid to a larger group of people, while at the same time rejuvenating the faith of the American congregation that hosted them. When we send people to Africa on short-term mission trips—often for just two weeks or less—only the few church members who travel get to see for themselves what is happening there. It would be more sensible to bring Africans here, surround them with the support of a church, and get to know them personally. It would make the African context come to life.

One potential outcome, however, is that when Africans come to the West, they will want to stay. This is of course understandable, especially if they come from a war-torn area, or a poverty-stricken region. For instance, our close friends hosted an Ethiopian boy named Werkinah in their home for a year. He came to America because of a terribly disfigured hand that would have prevented him from enjoying anything close to a normal life. An American discovered his situation, and a medical organization agreed to sponsor his numerous surgeries.

Over time Werkinah fell in love with American culture, learned to speak English, discovered a deep passion for basketball, and for the first time in his life was deeply valued by those around him. In his extremely poor Ethiopian village, his life was replete with rejection. In a society where secondary education is only for the upper classes, his future was rather dire since he was unable to perform the physical duties that most young men in an agricultural setting are expected to perform.

America, for Werkinah, was the land of opportunity. And he made the most of it. When the time came for him to return to Ethiopia, he didn't want to go. His life was much better here. His opportunities were virtually boundless in the United States. That was nearly ten years ago. Last I saw Werkinah, he was living with another family here in the States, doing whatever he could to remain here on a long-term basis. In America he saw hope and a future.

We have to be sensitive to what might happen when we cross boundaries. If we interact with people in Africa, or India, or other places in the global south, we must be prepared to face the consequences and responsibilities that might come with it. These consequences can be faced in one of two ways. We can see them as insurmountable problems, or we can choose to view them as full of potential and hope. I choose to do the latter.

I believe that when we get to know people from contexts unlike our own—especially if those contexts are poorer or more disadvantaged—tremendous hope is unleashed. We imagine possibilities that would never have arisen otherwise. We plant churches, build orphanages, give and receive education, learn to appreciate difference, and take one step closer to the kingdom envisioned in the New Testament:

You are no longer foreigners and strangers, but fellow citizens with God's people and also members of his household, built on the foundation of the apostles and

prophets, with Christ Jesus himself as the chief cornerstone. In him the whole building is joined together and
rises to become a holy temple in the Lord. (Ephesians
2:19–21)

When Paul wrote those words, it was a unique but challenging moment in time. Jews who put their faith in Christ
were learning how to open themselves up to Gentiles, joining
together with them in the building of the church. Similarly,
we in the West are today encountering new sisters and brothers in the global south, and together we can accomplish
much, that is, if we are able to accept them, and join with
them.

African Christianity: A Rich History

The story of Christianity's rise in Africa is an amazing one.
Some might think of it as a recent story, and in some ways it
is. Certainly, the growth of Christianity in Africa over the last
two centuries has been nothing short of spectacular. However, in other ways, Christianity has deep roots in Africa.
Indeed, those roots go way back to the time of Jesus, when
Mary and Joseph took their baby to Egypt and lived as
refugees for a period of time (Matthew 2:13–14). Yes, Jesus
lived in Africa.

But even before Jesus, the story of Israel intersects with
Africa at many points and in profound ways. God's people
were delivered from Egyptian bondage under the leadership
of Moses—the adopted son of an African monarch. In 1 Kings

10 we read about King Solomon's relationship with the Queen of Sheba (Ethiopia), a relationship that Ethiopians take very seriously because they believe a child—Menelik I—came out of that relationship and served as their first Solomonic emperor. Thus by the time of Jesus the African-Jewish connection was firmly established.

The book of Acts has no shortage of Africans. In Acts 2, during Pentecost, Libyans and Egyptians were present, right there at the birth of Christianity. A little later, in Acts 8, we read of an Ethiopian eunuch—an important official to the queen—who was on pilgrimage to Jerusalem and was reading the book of Isaiah. The apostle Philip shared the gospel with the African man, who immediately went into the water to be baptized. In Acts 11 evangelists from Cyrene (Libya) preached the gospel to Greeks in Antioch, and "the Lord's hand was with them" (Acts 11:21). In Acts 13:1–3 the apostle Paul was sent out on a mission trip by two men who were probably Africans: Simeon called Niger and Lucius of Cyrene. The respected evangelist Apollos was from Alexandria (Acts 18:24).

Africa's contribution to church history has been immense. According to tradition, it was the evangelist Mark who became the first head of the Coptic Orthodox Church (that is, Egyptian Orthodox). Saint Anthony the Great—the father of all monks—was Egyptian. Some of the greatest church fathers were Africans: Athanasius, Clement of Alexandria, Origen, Cyprian, Tertullian, and, of course, Augustine of Hippo—the father of Western Christian theology.

One of the world's first Christian nations was Ethiopia, which officially embraced Christianity as a state religion in the first half of the fourth century. Its ancient traditions give us a good sense of what Christianity must have looked like in the third and fourth centuries. Ethiopia's Debre Damo monastery is one of the oldest active monasteries in the world.[5]

Although Egypt and Ethiopia have a rich Christian heritage that goes back to early Christianity, in the fifteenth century Europeans became interested in evangelizing the rest of Africa. The Portuguese took the lead here and evangelized the kingdom of Kongo in the late fifteenth century, leading to many baptisms, including within the royal family. They expanded their evangelization into southern and eastern Africa during the sixteenth century through the efforts of many Catholic orders, including Carmelite nuns, Jesuits, Capuchins, and Dominicans. The promising missions fell to ruin, however, when the Portuguese began to exploit Africans for the burgeoning slave trade. Lamin Sanneh writes:

The sheer scale of this trade was unprecedented. From the mid-seventeenth century, tens of thousands of Africans were shipped off each year to plantations in the Americas. Portugal's African empire became primarily a

---

5. See Lamin Sanneh, "African Christianity: Historical and Thematic Horizons," in *The Wiley-Blackwell Companion to World Christianity*, ed. Lamin Sanneh and Michael McClymond (Oxford: John Wiley & Sons, 2016), 468.

source of slaves . . . slavers began seizing whole villages and devastating and depopulating entire districts.[6]

The end result was complete and utter social disintegration. Christianity was complicit in the disaster, and it is surprising that Africans in the slave-trade regions of Kongo and Angola ever gave Christianity another chance.

Protestants began doing mission work in Africa in the eighteenth century when the Society for the Propagation of the Gospel in Foreign Parts (SPG), a British organization, was established in 1701 for the purpose of global evangelization. By the end of the century several other nations got involved in the work, including the Netherlands, Germany, and Switzerland. During the nineteenth century, Protestant missions reached new heights due to the famed expeditions of the Scottish missionary David Livingstone. Although he was not an effective missionary, he opened the floodgates for Protestant missions to Africa, and waves of missionaries followed over the course of a century.

Over the last two centuries, the Christianization of sub-Saharan Africa has been complex. It is easy to emphasize the Western missionaries, but in reality those missionaries could have achieved little were it not for Africans who assisted them. Europeans could scarcely do the work of translation, navigating the terrain, preaching, or even finding food and clean water without the assistance of local Africans who accepted and looked after them. Already by early in the

6. Sanneh, "African Christianity," 475.

eighteenth century, Africans had become "the chief agents of Christianization."[7] There was little chance of Christianity succeeding in new lands otherwise, especially given the horrific slave era. Christianity was, unfortunately, complicit in the business of human trafficking, and it was difficult to differentiate Christianity and European imperialism. In the end, those first converts were able to make their case, and Christianity indigenized in the African continent.

African Christianity is not a carbon copy of Western Christianity. It has its own emphases, its own dynamics, and its own concerns. Despite the fact that Western denominations are strong in Africa, those churches are not pushed around by their Western counterparts.

For example, Namibia in southwest Africa has a population that is about half Lutheran, but by no means do those African Lutherans kowtow to Germany or Finland—the countries that missionized Namibia during colonial times. The Lutheran Church in Namibia has its own hierarchy. African nations usually enjoy good relations with the nations that formerly colonized them, but they are by no means subservient to them.

The same could be said for virtually all of Christian Africa. (The exception would be the Roman Catholic Church, where the pope is the primary authority; but that is not a situation unique to Africa.) Ever since African independence began in the 1950s, African Christian leadership has indigenized rapidly. When the Westerners left the continent, it was

---

7. Sanneh, "African Christianity," 482.

believed that Christianity might vanish with them. In reality, Christianity blossomed once the Europeans left.

Respected Kenyan theologian John Mbiti has described Africa's embrace of Christianity as being

> an African opportunity to mess up Christianity in our own way. For the past two thousand years, other continents, countries, nations and generations have had their chances to do with Christianity as they wished. And we know that they have not been idle! Now Africa has got its chance at last.[8]

Indeed, the twenty-first century should prove to be the African century for the Christian faith. Statistics show that Africa—already with over half a billion Christians—will surpass Latin America as the continent with the most Christians. Sub-Saharan Africa is poised to become a new Christendom due to its profoundly Christian character.

Today, Africa has fifty-nine countries and territories. In thirty-one of them, Christianity is the largest religion. Islam is dominant in twenty-one of them, and indigenous religions dominate in a handful of them. Basically Africa has a strongly Muslim north and a solidly Christian south. There are some nations in the center, such as Nigeria, that have strong Muslim *and* Christian populations and experience frequent conflict between the two.[9]

---

8. John Mbiti, quoted in Noel Davies and Martin Conway, *World Christianity in the 20th Century* (London: SCM, 2008), 118.

9. See Dyron Daughrity, *The Changing World of Christianity: The Global History of*

Christianity and Africa Rising Together

The twentieth century was a remarkable one for Christianity and Africa. In 1900, Africa only had about 10 million Christians. By mid-century, that number had increased to around 30 million. However, by century's end, there were nearly 500 million Christians in Africa. Today, Africans account for around 20 percent of the world's Christians.[10] And considering that fertility rates are much higher in Africa than in the rest of the world, that figure will rise.

What this means is that as world Christianity becomes more African, we will see a more profoundly African influence on the faith. In ways, we are coming full circle. Early Christianity was dominated by African intellectuals such as Athanasius and Augustine, and these towering figures influenced Christian theology profoundly. Africa's impact on twenty-first-century Christianity might be equally as strong.

Today we are witnessing Africa's influence on certain global denominations such as the Anglican Communion, which is undergoing a shift in leverage as African clerics assume their leadership role. It is undeniable that the future of global Anglicanism is an African one. Already there are far more Anglicans in Nigeria than in England, and Africa claims around 60 percent of the world's 90 million Anglicans. The Anglican Church's future would be in great peril were it not for their African counterparts.[11]

a Borderless Religion (New York: Peter Lang, 2010). Statistics for that book come directly from two sources: the *World Christian Database* and the *CIA World Factbook*.

10. Terence Ranger, ed., *Evangelical Christianity and Democracy in Africa* (Oxford: Oxford University Press, 2008), ix–x.

Christianity's rise in Africa should continue because new varieties of the faith blossom almost daily. What is remarkable about African Christianity is that it is so young and vibrant. It is not associated mainly with the elderly generations as we see in the Western world. Rather, it is strongly employed by the youth. Christianity is something people are excited about. It is not a relic of the past, as it is in parts of Europe. Rather it holds great promise. It is something new and fresh, full of promise and adventure. It is a relatively new faith in much of Africa, and young people gravitate towards it.

World Christianity is benefiting tremendously from Africa's embrace of the religion. We are seeing Christianity through new lenses at it moves to the global south. And as Christianity's center of gravity moves toward Africa, we will see the Christian agenda dominated more by issues associated with the developing world: extreme poverty, high unemployment, disease, war-torn nations, refugees, famine, and utter reliance on God. The so-called "Enlightenment" in the West called into question many biblical and spiritual ideas, but in the African context those concepts are very much in play: demons, exorcism, fasting, witchcraft, healing, miracles, and the power of the Holy Spirit.

African Christianity is full of momentum. Churches are being planted all over, and they mushroom quickly. Church attendance is considered vital for practicing Christians. It

11. See the BBC article "Anglican Church around the World," 15 July 2008: http://news.bbc.co.uk/2/hi/3226753.stm. See also "Global Anglicanism at a Crossroads," Pew Forum on Religion and Public Life, 19 June 2008, located at http://www.pewforum.org/Christian/Global-Anglicanism-at-a-Crossroads.aspx.

would be unthinkable for most African Christians to attend church only on Christmas and Easter and perhaps a few Sundays in between. Christian gatherings occur daily, both formal and informal. People's lives are organized around their church involvement, and when one misses services, the pastor or a deacon will come around to make sure everything is okay. Religion is taken very seriously in Africa, for it has the power to help people in life's daily struggles.

In Africa, pastors are greatly respected. They are seen as individuals with divine gifts who can truly help a community to rise up. Pastors are trusted deeply because they exert power over evil, they are chosen by God, and they are perceived as being capable of improving people's lives both spiritually and physically. I once heard Philip Jenkins say that, in America, we are suspicious of pastors who claim they cast out demons. But in Africa, people are suspicious of pastors who *cannot* cast out demons.

And while African Christianity is rising remarkably, in some places on the continent it is not easy to be a Christian. A case in point is Egypt. In the last few years, stories of violent attacks against Coptic Christians have been in the news frequently. It has been truly impressive to see their unity, steadfastness, and Christ-like qualities in the face of calamity.

In February 2015 the world was horrified to learn of twenty-one Coptic construction workers in Libya who were kidnapped and beheaded by ISIS. In May 2016 gunmen stopped a Coptic bus full of pilgrims heading to a monastery retreat, emptied it, and executed at least twenty-eight people, a group that included children. In December 2016 a bomb was detonated in the Coptic cathedral, leaving at least twenty-five Christians dead. In April 2017, on Palm Sunday, ISIS coordinated two church bombings in Tanta and Alexandria that left forty-four Coptic Christians dead and dozens severely injured. These stories have become common in Egypt, but the response and resolve of the Coptic Christians is inspiring. As a church, they have chosen the path of forgiveness rather than retaliation. In the aftermath of the Palm Sunday massacres, a prominent Egyptian talk show host struggled to comprehend the Coptic response to the violence: "The Copts of Egypt . . . are made of . . . steel!"[12]

African Christians are not only resilient, but they are also far more charismatic in their worship than Westerners are. A strong Pentecostal ethos lives in the African Independent Churches (or AICs, as they are often called). The AICs have little to no connection to denominations in the Western world, and they are the churches that are growing most dramatically. We certainly see Catholicism and Anglicanism growing in Africa, but this is due largely to high fertility rates. Where we see the most remarkable growth is within these independent churches that lean heavily in the Pentecostal direction. The Pentecostal approach to Christianity is so popular in Africa that older denominations such as the

---

12. Jayson Casper, "Forgiveness: Muslims Moved as Coptic Christians Do the Unimaginable," *Christianity Today*, 20 April 2017, located at http://www.christianityto-day.com/news/2017/april/forgiveness-muslims-moved-coptic-christians-egypt-isis.html.

Roman Catholic Church are now incorporating charismatic elements in order to meet the high demand.[13]

Typically, the African Independent Churches are led by pastors who are identified by their faith community as being prophets. This notion of prophethood has roots in colonial Africa, when charismatic preachers like William Wade Harris and Simon Kimbangu began churches that still carry their name. Indeed the Harrist churches have hundreds of thousands of members in West Africa. The Kimbanguist numbers are today in the millions, and both groups are official members of the World Council of Churches.[14]

Pentecostalism plays a key role in the phenomenal growth of Christianity in Africa, and some of the movement's pastors have become superstars in the African Christian constellation. For example, William Kumuyi's Deeper Life Bible Church in Nigeria has a membership of around 800,000.[15] The International Central Gospel Church in Accra, Ghana, founded in the 1980s, has thousands of members and one of the most respected educational institutions in the country: Central University. Nigerian megachurch pastor David Oyedepo is probably the most recognized African pastor due to the tremendous success of the church he founded: Winner's Chapel. It is a profoundly successful network of churches

13. See, for example, John Allen Jr., "Pentecostal, Evangelical boom forces African Church to 'wake up,'" *Crux*, 25 March 2017, located at https://cruxnow.com/africaund/2017/03/25/pentecostal-evangelical-boom-forces-african-church-wake/.
14. See the list of WCC member churches at https://www.oikoumene.org/en/member-churches/.
15. See Tiwaloba Abidemi Falaye, "The History and Practices of Deeper Life Bible Church (Nigeria)," *Journal of Philosophy, Culture and Religion* 8 (2015), located at http://iiste.org/Journals/index.php/JPCR/article/view/23416/23843.

located in three hundred cities, both in Africa and beyond. In 2011, *Forbes* magazine named Pastor Oyedepo the wealthiest Nigerian pastor—quite an accomplishment considering that many Nigerian pastors have become multimillionaires. His net worth is estimated to be well over $150 million.[16]

Pentecostalism has been criticized widely for what is perceived to be an overemphasis on prosperity.[17] However, Westerners cannot fully relate to the African context where one's life can slip into crisis suddenly. Africans value prosperity as a sign of God's favor. It is affirmation that they have made good choices, and God blesses their efforts to please him. This is not a concept wholly foreign in the West, but the two contexts are quite different. Most Westerners enjoy a social safety net that can help them during times of struggle. Most Africans, however, have no such safety net, and thus rely on their church for deliverance.

While it may appear to a Western eye that the African emphasis on prosperity smacks of greed, the fact is that prosperity in the African context is not solely about money. It is about deliverance from hostile forces, about having employment, about health, about release from bondage and curses, and about the greatest blessing one can enjoy—children. Indeed a large family is a sign of God's favor in the African context, a concept reinforced by their reading of the Bible.[18] This is one of the key reasons that polygamy continues in

16. Mfonobong Nsehe, "The Five Richest Pastors in Nigeria," *Forbes*, 7 June 2011, located at https://www.forbes.com/sites/mfonobongnsehe/2011/06/07/the-five-richest-pastors-in-nigeria/#71fd804d6031.

17. California pastor John MacArthur is one of the more vocal critics of Pentecostalism.

18. For more on African Pentecostalism, see Kwabena Asamoah-Gyadu, "African

many parts of Africa. A man with multiple wives and numerous children has quite obviously received divine favor.

While Pentecostalism gets criticized for its emphasis on health and wealth, in the African context, one's theology is judged by its practical effects. And people believe strongly in God's ability to help them. I once heard a Pentecostal woman pastor declare, "When people are in need, we are the last that they approach, but we are the first to solve their problems." There is a widespread sense that church leaders are competent in their ability to help people. And in a context where decent healthcare can be elusive, people turn to their religious leaders.

When Ebola struck West Africa a few years ago, many Nigerians—including health officials—turned to T. B. Joshua, the head pastor of the Synagogue Church of All Nations, a congregation of some fifty thousand members. Joshua was a lightning rod for criticism during the Ebola outbreak because many people went to him for healing or prevention, *instead of* turning to local health officials. While some of the professionals criticized him, others realized that his influence was so profound they *had* to work with him. Joshua took a middle path in his response. He urged Christians to avoid travel so as not to spread the disease—actually officials had urged him to take such a position. However, he also demonstrated great confidence in his ability to offer healing in the name of Christ when he commissioned four thousand bottles of

Pentecostal/Charismatic Christianity: An Overview," *Lausanne World Pulse* 8 (2006), located at https://www.lausanneworldpulse.com/themedarticles-php/464/08-2006.

anointed water to be sent to Sierra Leone. In Africa, "There's the perception that Christianity works better than any of the alternatives." And it seems as if Pastor Joshua has this figured out.[19]

African Christianity presents us with a series of contrasts. Christianity is ancient there, yet its explosive growth is more recent. In the nineteenth and first half of the twentieth centuries, Africa was a place to send missionaries. Since independence, that situation has changed. In the last two decades, Africa has become a land that sends out missionaries of its own, usually through migration. Africa glows with a bright Christian hope for the future.

African Christianity is rising. In the twentieth century, Christianity in Africa skyrocketed from about 10 percent of the continent's population to around half. However, numbers reveal only the tip of the iceberg. Christianity is in its heyday in Africa. For many, Christianity is a relatively new religion, something that took the continent by storm. In only a century the Christian faith morphed from marginal to majority status. The reverberations of Christianity's rise there will be with us for a long time. It will be fascinating to observe how Christianity continues to shape Africa, but perhaps more fascinating will be how world Christianity gets shaped *by* Africa.

---

19. Sunday Oguntola and Ruth Moon, "Why Nigerian Health Officials Turned to a Megachurch Pastor When Ebola Struck," *Christianity Today*, 29 October 2014, located at http://www.christianitytoday.com/ct/2014/november/ebola-tb-joshua-healing.html.

6

Embracing Christ in Asia

As a PhD student at the University of Calgary in Canada, I had just finished my Comprehensive Exams—a series of written and oral exams meant to determine whether a student should be allowed to start working on their dissertation. My supervisor and I sat down for a lengthy discussion of what I should spend the next three years researching. I can still recall details from that meeting.

He had actually invited one of his old mentors to meet with us. We talked about my academic strengths and desires, and what topics had already been covered. We explored several possibilities until settling on the topic of Stephen Charles Neill—a well-known British bishop who worked in India in the first half of the twentieth century. The meeting was moving along really well until my supervisor said to me, "Okay, you'll need to spend some time in India to do your field research."

It had not occurred to me before that I'd actually have to

go there. Initially I figured I could just spend my time in the library, ordering materials on interlibrary loan. No, he said, must settle in India for a while, find a place to stay, and get the required materials in order to write something new, something that was actually considered a contribution to scholarship. If I was diligent, he estimated, I could probably get what I needed in two or three months.

I was excited, but intimidated. I knew very little about India, other than basic information about religion there. But to actually fly there, travel around in sleeper trains, and plant myself in a completely foreign culture . . . that was lunacy. Wasn't it? I didn't know anybody in India. Not one person!

So I did it. As a PhD student you have no other choice. You just learn to say yes. Within a few months I was India bound, on a painfully long flight, with very little sense of what to expect.

Thus began my love affair with a country that I have come to appreciate deeply. And over the years I have been privileged to travel to other Asian nations. Each has a unique history. Religiously, Asian nations are extremely diverse. For example, Japan is Shinto mixed with Buddhist. Indonesia and Malaysia are mainly Muslim. Christianity is strong in South Korea and the Philippines. India is majority Hindu. China is complex, with an emphasis on Buddhism and Taoism, although virtually everybody has been impacted by the teachings of Confucius. Southeast Asia (Vietnam, Laos, Cambodia, Thailand, Myanmar) is primarily Buddhist.

And while globalization is bringing Asians and Western

people closer together through technology, trade, and the widely spoken English language, Asia can still be disorienting for Westerners. It certainly was for me.

The Vast Potential for Christianity in India

Life in rural India is dramatically different from Western culture. It is virtually impossible for a Westerner to enter an Indian village without having an accompanying Indian who can help out. It is just so vastly different from what we are used to: mud huts, language barriers, unique customs and taboos, and a deeply entrenched social system based on caste that foreigners struggle to comprehend.

I have spent a good amount of time in India. I did my doctoral field work there, taught in a college, led a study-abroad program, and still return every two or three years to continue with my own research. I have meaningful friendships there, and as strange as the culture is for me, I have grown to cherish it and its impact on my life. India has taught me much about myself. It is ironic how a culture so dramatically different from ours can be so beautiful yet so challenging at the same time.

During my first trip to India I was confronted with true poverty at my first stop—the city of Calcutta, now called Kolkata. The city has inherited the nickname City of Joy, even though many people are destitute and desperately poor. It's no wonder Mother Teresa decided to base her ministry in the downtown sector of this city.

Kolkata has so many people who are in dire need. I remember walking the streets with a Hindu man. We were literally stepping over sickly and dying people when I asked him what could be done to fix this awful situation. He explained that while it is truly sad, they would be reborn and would have another chance at life. He said he hoped they would make good decisions in their next life so they could avoid the consequences that they currently find themselves in. Of course I had read about reincarnation and the Hindu understanding of rebirth, but it became all too real for me that day as we stepped over dozens of people lying on the sidewalks, people who urgently needed assistance.

Mother Teresa's place is known locally as the Mother House. Every taxi driver knows where it is. When I visited for the first time in 2001, I was deeply moved. Her tomb is the holiest place I have ever been. Here was one woman's attempt to give her life to this cause. Mother Teresa persistently endeavored to make a difference despite the fact that she could never fix the deeply rooted problems there. Freely she gave herself to those living on the streets in appalling conditions, people who had no one else to turn to. This tiny, devout, humble nun from Macedonia based her ministry in one of the most painfully hopeless places on earth.

Mother Teresa died in 1997 at the age of eighty-seven, but she left an amazing legacy, called the Missionaries of Charity, a religious order she founded in 1950 at the age of forty. She was a lifeline to prostitutes, lepers, orphans, AIDS patients, elderly people without family, refugees, the mentally ill, the sick, and the dying. With outstretched arms, she took people's faces into her hands and spoke encouragement to them. She was fearless, considering the fact that some of the people she ministered to were contagious, or mentally unstable.

After her death it was revealed in her diary that she occasionally struggled with her faith. It was difficult for her to understand why God allowed such suffering, and why so few people actually tried to help them.

Mother Teresa exemplified true Christian devotion. She abandoned everything for the sake of the gospel. She took Christ's teachings extremely seriously, and in 2016 was recognized as a saint by the Roman Catholic Church. Her impact, however, goes far beyond the Catholic orbit. She was loved deeply in India, and was honored many times by the nation. Indeed, all the world came to know her and her good works.

Mother Teresa's work is emblematic of Christianity in India. She worked hard to be a witness and example for Christ, but with little payoff in terms of Christian converts. Her Missionaries of Charity still excel in charitable works, but they have accomplished little if we measure the success of a missionary only by the number of baptisms.

Over the last several centuries, so many Christian missionaries spent their careers in India with comparatively few results. In Africa, the people responded en masse, and in only a century Christianity rose to majority status. That did not happen in India, where Christianity represents only about 3 to 5 percent of the population.

There are many theories as to why Christianity has not caught on in India, at least not on a large scale. Some blame the caste system, saying that when the outcastes began turning to Christ, they caused high-ranked castes to look down on Christianity. It was becoming a religion for the poor and marginalized. There are significant cultural taboos against low-caste people in India. The upper castes are not supposed to deal directly with them, based on old laws of ritual purity—laws that have been officially condemned, but that definitely persist in the cultural ethos.

Others blame the era of European colonialism for the low numbers of Indians turning to Christ. When the British seized power, they created an unbridgeable cultural chasm between themselves and the local people. Indians resented being ruled by a small group of officials located on some far distant island in the Western world.

Others have blamed Christian division. They say that while Hindus are united by their religion, Christians in India are fragmented into many different sects. If you join Christianity, you essentially join a fractious and contentious religion that cares more for upholding its sectarian preferences than uniting with others.

In some ways these critiques ring true. Indeed Indian Christians have split into many different groups and subgroups, but they are merely a reflection of the state of world Christianity. Many missionaries established churches in India that are distrustful of one another—caring more about upholding the tenets of their own sect than adapting Christianity to Indian culture. They tried to plant a Western form of the faith without regard for local customs.

Indians admire and respect Jesus Christ. They understand why Christians built a religion around this peaceful teacher and miracle worker who was sent by God. The notion of avatars is a concept that most Indians take for granted. They have no problem believing in a God-man who was sent to earth to bring peace and save humans from their own sins, delivering them from the power of evil. Hinduism also has stories of gods coming to earth, trying to help humanity.

Where Indians have objections, however, is with the behavior of Christians. The common complaint is that Christians don't act like Christ. It was this disparity that led to Mahatma Gandhi's observation that "Christians, missionaries and all, must begin to live more like Jesus Christ."[1]

Gandhi was no enemy to Christianity; he just believed Christians should follow Christ more carefully, and more faithfully. Gandhi held Jesus in very high esteem, and understood his teachings well. In fact, many of Gandhi's core ideas were inspired by Jesus, for example passive resistance and turning the other cheek. Gandhi was able to persuade the British to leave India without ever inciting violence. In fact he condemned violence, promoting instead the teaching of Jesus that one should not resist an evil person (Matthew 5:39). Indeed, a Hindu leader once said, "I never understood the meaning of Christianity until I saw it in Gandhi."[2]

1. E. Stanley Jones, *Gandhi: Portrayal of a Friend* (Nashville: Abingdon, 1948), 51–52.
2. E. Stanley Jones, *The Christ of the Indian Road* (London: Hodder & Stoughton, 1925), 101.

153

Fundamentally, I don't think the problem is that Indians have rejected the teachings of Jesus. Many of the great gurus in Indian history said many of the same things that Jesus did. The Buddha taught often on compassion, and on the equality of all human beings. These are aspects of Christianity that Indians welcome.

The problem is the baggage that Christians have often brought with them. The Portuguese came in search of spices and were reckless in their dealings with locals, as happened in the Americas as well. The British managed to get virtually all of India under their control, causing lasting resentment. But these governments also sponsored Christian missions. And it was often difficult for Indians to understand the difference between colonialism and Christianity. If Christianity was a religion intent on domination and subjugation, then they wanted no part of it.

One of my closest friends is an Indian seminary professor and a Pentecostal pastor. His name is V. V. Thomas and he teaches theology and church history at Union Biblical Seminary in Pune, a city of around three million people in the state of Maharashtra, not far from Bombay. V. V. is a well-known figure in the Indian seminary context. He is a jovial man, always ready to break the ice with a turn of phrase or a joke. He is a sincere Christian, eager to stay up late, sitting on the floor of a hotel room, praying out loud in Malayalam—his mother tongue. I know this to be true because I have had to use earplugs while he prayed with all his might—often past midnight—during our travels together.

In 2014, V. V. and I traveled to several different seminaries to conduct a study on seminary education in India. We interviewed faculty and students at Orthodox, Catholic, mainline Protestant, Evangelical, and Pentecostal institutions of higher education. It was a tremendous learning experience, in spite of the fact that many of the divisions in Western Christianity have been transferred to the Indian context through denominationally funded mission enterprises.

It is difficult to be a Christian in many parts of India. According to the 2011 census, India is only 2.3 percent Christian. That means there are around thirty million Christians in the nation. However, that number is very likely higher because many Indians are under pressure to hide their Christian faith due to religious stigma. The Indian government has an affirmative action program called Reservation that is available for some disadvantaged social groups. However, the socially disadvantaged—known in India as Dalits—are typically only eligible for these benefits if they are from an Indian-born religion, which means Hinduism, Buddhism, and Sikhism. Thus, the poorer Christian communities struggle to break out of their poverty because they are ineligible to apply for government positions that would give them a measure of financial stability and provide opportunities for social advancement.

Disadvantaged Indian Christians, however, take matters into their own hands by developing Christian schools, orphanages, medical clinics, and other institutions aimed at their own social uplift. My friend V. V. has established a small,

all-male Bible school in the state of Kerala called Focus India Theological College. In my time spent with the young men of this theological college, I have been impressed by their determined commitment to learning English, to understanding Christian ministry and theology, and to living a disciplined Christian life in a culture that does not always reward their efforts. Some of the students travel from 1,800 miles away just to get a chance to improve their lives as well as the lives of their families who have placed so much hope in them.

In America, we often think of the parents as the ones who have resources, and they are expected to take care of their children well into their twenties, if not longer. In India, it is the reverse. The children are usually the ones that bear the burden of looking after the parents. Parents rely on their children to take care of them into their twilight years.

It has been very encouraging for me to witness the number of young people who are training for ministry in India. Many of them face an uncertain future, however. They will be like the farmer in the parable of the sower, whose seeds often fall onto dry ground, and get choked by weeds or eaten by birds. Indian ministers may toil for years and have only a small house church of two or three families to show for all of their efforts. But these committed disciples did not choose to go into ministry for material reasons. Rather, they are interested in seeing Christianity's harvest rise up in a place that has been closed to the gospel.

Under certain conditions, Christianity does occasionally blossom in India. There are several megachurches in India, for instance New Life Fellowship in Mumbai, which claims to have two thousand services in two hundred different locations weekly.[3] With 130,000 members, Calvary Temple in Hyderabad has been called "the world's fastest-growing congregation."[4] What is surprising is how quickly it grew; the church was founded only in 2005. Full Gospel Assembly of God in Bangalore claims 17,000 attendees and 300 million television viewers per week.[5] And there are others, such as the Bethel Assembly of God Church in Bangalore and the Mark Buntain Memorial Assembly of God Church in Kolkata. These churches defy the notion that Christianity doesn't work in India. These churches are trailblazers, showing that Christianity's rise in Asia might finally be including India.

India is a nation that Americans should pay more attention to, especially considering that tens of millions of Indians are fluent in English. This is an important fact. It is far more difficult to communicate with people of most other Asian nations. India's strong English-speaking skills present American Christians with vast opportunities for getting to know them, working with them, and sharing the good news of Jesus with them.

India is also a place where religion is taken very seriously. Indians appreciate faith, and are very open to hearing the

---

3. See http://www.nlfa.org/.
4. See Michael Brown, "7 Lessons from the World's Fastest Growing Congregation," *The Christian Post*, 13 December 2015, located at http://www.christianpost.com/news/7-lessons-from-the-worlds-fastest-growing-congregation-152310/.
5. See Imchen Sungjemmeren, "Indian Megachurches' Centripetal Mission," *Lausanne World Pulse*, January 2011, located at https://www.lausanneworldpulse.com/perspectives-php/1360/01-2011.

gospel. It is fascinating to imagine what might happen if India—soon to be the most populous nation on earth—began turning to Christ on a large scale.

Korea: The Land of Megachurches

For many years I aspired to attend worship services at Yoido Full Gospel Church, the largest Christian congregation in the world. Finally in 2013 I had my chance when I attended the World Council of Churches assembly in the beautiful, coastal city of Busan, South Korea. They gave us options for a cultural exposure experience. It was clear to me that I must go to Seoul and see for myself how this massive church operates.

Yoido is run with marvelous efficiency. With 800,000 members, everything is planned down to the minute. When one service ends, the people are expected to get right up and head for the door as another group files into the sanctuary. It is like clockwork, but can present a challenge to those who want to get a seat in one of their eighteen weekly services. The church was founded in 1958, and moved to its present location in 1973. So they have had time to figure out how to make it work.

Yoido Full Gospel Church is a member of the Assemblies of God—a Pentecostal denomination founded in 1914 in the United States. However, even in a denomination associated with megachurches, this one is staggering. They have twenty-eight chapels at the facility. They have planted 447 churches in Korea alone. Members gather weekly in one of the church's 9632 cell groups. They are led by 410 pastors on staff and 1,205 elders. They have 14,439 deacons and 35,176 deaconesses, plus an additional 10,476 Senior Deacons and Deaconesses. Their foreign-language worship services are reminiscent of a small United Nations conference.[6] Yoido is not just big in terms of numbers; they have big ministries that help people's lives. They are deeply committed to the work of education. They operate secular as well as religious schools, conduct ministry training, and offer courses for new Christian converts as well as more advanced theology programs. They provide vocational education for teens and young adults. They run a Christian university (Hansei) in Korea as well as one in California (Bethesda). They have their own seminary (Youngsan), and oversee a massive preschool center.

Yoido also operates many medical assistance programs in various Asian nations. Their social welfare programs are impressive, including work with the unemployed and with seniors. One of their ministries—Elim Welfare Town—has a budget of $1.5 billion. Their work in North Korea is extensive and includes a soybean factory, children's meal service, a corn seed program, fertilizer provisions, grain powder for the North Korean public school system, and a tuberculosis treatment initiative. They provide advanced medical procedures to heart patients in North Korea for free.

In my view, the best hope for Korean unification is not found in military saber rattling or diplomacy; rather, the

---

6. Accurate statistics for this legendary church are hard to come by. Some people have claimed the church is over a million members. My information is from the official booklet I received at the church, titled *Yoido Full Gospel Church*.

unification of the peninsula will take place only when trust is rebuilt through loving concern and good-faith measures such as what Yoido is doing. Good deeds offered in genuine love can eventually thaw the coldest of hearts.

Yoido Full Gospel Church is by no means the only massive church in Korea. Of the fifty largest churches in the world, South Korea is home to about half of them.[7] The nation has so many mega-churches that they are not even considered to be megachurches until they have over ten thousand members.

South Korea's Christian explosion has several historical causes. Korea was under Japanese control from 1905 to 1945, a brutal period in Korean history. When I visited Korea in 2013, I attended a major drama-musical at 100,000-member Myungsung Presbyterian Church in Seoul—the largest Presbyterian church in the world. It was scathing in its portrayal of the period of Japanese occupation, and glowing in its representation of Americans, especially American missionaries. South Koreans deeply appreciate America, and its tremendous help throughout the twentieth century. In the musical I saw, the American missionaries were lauded as dedicated people who had Korea's best interests in mind—they looked like heroes.

Christianity trickled into Korea during the seventeenth, eighteenth, and nineteenth centuries, often through Korean diplomats who encountered Jesuits or perhaps some of their converts. Christianity's popularity increased in the late nine-

---

7. Sebastian C. H. Kim, "Mega Churches in South Korea: Their Impact and Prospect in the Public Sphere," in *A Moving Faith: Mega Churches Go South*, ed. Jonathan James (Los Angeles: Sage, 2015), 85.

teenth century when Protestants established numerous schools in the nation. The Protestant approach was brilliant. It was taken straight out of St. Francis Xavier's playbook: a focus on educating children. However, things would soon change in dramatic fashion.

The Japanese took control of Korea in 1905, damaging Korea's connection to the Western world. It was a brutal time. Any Korean dissent or opposition to Japanese colonialism was crushed.

When World War II ended in 1945, Korea was split into two. When the Japanese left, the Soviet Union took control of the north and turned it into a Communist satellite state. The United States took charge of the south. At that point, Christians made up less than 5 percent of the population. However, during the late 1940s, "there was a strong movement toward making South Korea a Christian nation . . . built on the basis of the Bible and on Christ, the Rock."[8]

The first president of South Korea, Syngman Rhee, was a Christian and an avid supporter of the United States. He studied at George Washington University, Harvard, and Princeton between 1905 and 1910. He served as president of South Korea for twelve years, from 1948 to 1960, and made an enormous impact on the nation, although sometimes through questionable means. He incorporated Christian rituals into government ceremonies, and he promoted Christians to important positions in his government, in spite of the fact that Christianity was the chosen religion of only about

8. Kim, "Mega Churches in South Korea," 87.

5 percent of the national population at the time. All of these things set the tone for Christian growth, especially in the political realm.[9]

During the Korean War (1950–1953), President Rhee gave preferential treatment to Protestants, particularly through his adoption of a military chaplaincy program in 1951. These Protestant chaplains planted Christianity in the military ranks, and many soldiers turned to Christ. President Rhee's vision for a Protestant nation, much like the United States that he so loved and admired, began to come to form. He was ousted in a military coup, however, and fled to Hawaii, where he died in 1965.

By the 1960s, South Korea and the United States had developed an extraordinarily close relationship. America was seen as the nation that ended the Japanese colonial era, and also came to their aid during the Korean War—a war that helped them to remain free and democratic rather than social- ist. Today, the legacy of America's involvement in South Korea is clear, especially in comparison to North Korea.

Korean Christianity is so lively and active because of its unique history. South Koreans are mindful of what could have been, had history played out differently. They are a nation that began turning to Christ very recently, and have watched their nation rise up from the ashes, with Christianity rising up alongside it. Christianity is associated with South Korea's good fortune in recent decades.

My mother visited South Korea in 1964 as a performer

9. Kim, "Mega Churches in South Korea," 87.

in the USO (United Services Organization). She was with a group of American university students who traveled around Asia singing and dancing for American troops in Korea, Japan, Taiwan, Guam, and the Philippines. I asked her about what she saw in 1964 and she said it was an extremely rural nation except for Seoul. She noticed makeshift shelters everywhere on the streets, which was a shock to her. These people were homeless. She remembers riding in the bus, overlooking miles of rice fields, with a strong stench in the air due to animal waste being used for fertilizer. It was a very poor nation, trying to rebuild in the aftermath of an international war that had reduced it to rubble.

After visiting Korea in 2013, I enjoyed talking with my mom about how much the nation had changed. The Korea I experienced was just as developed as America, perhaps even more so: numerous skyscrapers, luxury cars on the streets, classy restaurants, and, yes, megachurches that dwarf virtually all of the churches in the Western world. It is hard to believe that only a generation ago South Korea was a struggling, developing nation known more for its war wreckage than for its stellar education system and technology boom.

South Korea's unexpected embrace of Christianity is as impressive as its rapid economic advancement. And the key to Korean Christianity's rise has been its independence from foreign supervision. From early on, the American missionaries discouraged Koreans from relying on American money. They were encouraged to build their churches themselves.

Throughout the twentieth century, many missionary

programs created a climate of dependency with the churches they planted abroad. Still today there are churches in the global south that depend on America for support, sometimes for many decades after they were established. Koreans have taken the opposite approach. They took charge of their churches themselves, resisting any kind of dependency on the U.S., other than moral support. And not only did they become self-supporting, but they also became self-propagating. South Korea sends more Christian missionaries abroad than any other country, except for the U.S.

Christians today account for nearly a third of the South Korean population. The churches grew impressively throughout the twentieth century, but of course, they still face problems. For example, there have been some high-profile corruption cases in Korean megachurches, including an embezzlement scandal that rocked the Yoido congregation and landed the lead pastor's son in prison.[10] Nevertheless, I believe the South Korean churches will learn from these mistakes, and will continue to serve as the epicenter of Asian missions for years to come.

Unleashing the Gospel in China

China is the biggest story in global Christianity today. While estimates vary, it is quite possible that China is home to some 100 million Christians.[11] If that is indeed the case, then on any

---

10. Ruth Moon, "Founder of World's Largest Megachurch Convicted of Embezzling Million," *Christianity Today*, 24 February 2014, located at http://www.christianity-today.com/news/2014/february/founder-of-worlds-largest-megachurch-convicted-cho-yoido.html.

given Sunday there are more Chinese attending church than Americans.

It is difficult to fathom how much China has changed over the last generation. For Christians, the changes are most certainly for the better. After centuries of very modest success, Christianity is finally catching on. If it continues to grow, then this could be an epochal moment in the history of Christianity.

The Christians of China endured a brutal twentieth century. During the reign of Mao Zedong (ruled 1945–1976) religion was suppressed. Missionaries were sent home, church leaders were humiliated and imprisoned, and all church buildings were put to secular use. Untold numbers were martyred for their faith. However, like the story of the phoenix, Christianity has a way of rising from the ashes. And in the last few decades, Christianity's upward momentum in China has been pronounced.

Chinese Christianity is organized into recognized and unrecognized churches. The recognized churches operate legally but are subject to government oversight. This causes resentment from some of the unrecognized Christian groups—known often as house churches or as underground churches (although they are not located underground). Simply put, China's house churches are not registered with the government, thus they risk censure or even closure at any time. They are usually smaller churches, consisting of

11. For the range of estimates of how many Christians are in China, see Pew Forum's research methodology, located at http://www.pewforum.org/files/2011/12/ChristianityAppendixC.pdf.

anywhere between a few dozen to several hundred members. It has become increasingly common for people to actually attend both a house church (unrecognized) as well as an officially registered church without any sense of conflict.

Christians in China who are members of house churches have been known to be persecuted, but rarely are the persecutions violent. Government authorities might reprimand the pastor, or perhaps prohibit them from meeting at a certain property. In those cases the churches simply ask members to start meeting elsewhere. More severe crackdowns, however, have accelerated in recent years. Incarceration for unregistered Christians has picked up since 2014, when 2,994 Christians were reportedly detained and 1,274 sentenced to jail time.[12]

The registered churches receive government funding for buildings and for the education of their pastors. Their congregations are often in the thousands. The Chinese government allows the following religions to exist: Daoism, Buddhism, Islam, Catholicism, and Protestantism. However, they are carefully supervised by the State Administration for Religious Affairs.[13]

I am personally acquainted with China's ambivalence toward religion. In 2016 I signed a contract with a public university in China to teach two courses on World Religions during the summer of 2017. However, a week before I

---

12. See "China Aid 2014 Annual Report," 21 April 2015, located at http://www.chinaaid.org/2015/04/china-aid-2014-annual-report-indicates.html.
13. See Eleanor Albert, "Religion in China," *Council on Foreign Relations*, 10 June 2015, located at https://www.cfr.org/backgrounder/religion-china.

departed, the university sent me an emergency notice that the contract had been unexpectedly canceled. The letter specified that the "Ministry of Education has tightened the policy on setting up religions courses in Chinese Universities so that our university is not allowed to open religions courses taught by foreigners anymore."[14] I was told that this was a new policy that went into effect immediately. The people who hired me were as shocked by the news as I was, and apologized sincerely. They tried to negotiate with the higher-ups, but to no avail.

In comparison to the brutal oppression of the 1960s and 70s, China's attitude toward religion has loosened up significantly. However, it is important to keep in mind two things: first, China is a Communist nation, with a one-party system. And second, the Communist party is *officially* atheist. That doesn't mean that all Communists are atheists, but it does mean that Communists must be careful about revealing too much about their personal beliefs. If their beliefs do not measure up with the Communist platform, then they have much to lose, and they could certainly be dismissed from their government job. David Aikman, the former *Time* magazine Beijing bureau chief, has revealed that despite the stakes, Christians are in all levels of the Chinese government. They just keep their faith to themselves.[15]

China's rapidly expanding Christian population is due partly to politics. Christianity is associated with democracy,

---

14. Personal email dated 22 June 2017.
15. David Aikman, *Jesus in Beijing* (Washington, DC: Regnery, 2003), 8–11.

more civil rights, and more openness toward the rest of the world. The Tiananmen Square protests of 1989 were led by a number of young adults, many of whom were Christians. After a period of suppression in the 1990s, the government resumed an attitude of openness in the 2000s, a trajectory that has had very favorable consequences for Christianity's growth in China.

In China, Christianity is associated with the Western world, where freedom, democracy, and capitalism prevail. And while China has clearly embraced capitalism, there are signs that democracy and increased personal freedoms are percolating just under the surface. There are certainly bumps in the road for Christians in the nation. It is not uncommon to hear of sporadic persecution.

For example, between 2014 and 2016 there was a large-scale "decapitation" of churches in China, specifically in the province of Zhejiang, where Christianity has made huge strides in recent years.[16] The government removed their crowning red crosses, which are often lit up at night so they can be seen from miles away. Estimates are that up to 1,700 churches had their crosses torn down. The city of Wenzhou, often called the Chinese Jerusalem because of its 1.3 million Christians, was hit particularly hard by the purge.[17]

16. See Ian Johnson, "Decapitated Churches in China's Christian Heartland," *New York Times*, 21 May 2016, located at https://www.nytimes.com/2016/05/22/world/asia/china-christians-zhejiang.html?_r=0.
17. For Wenzhou's Christian population, see Sarah Eekhoff Zylstra, "China Sees Red," *Christianity Today*, 3 August 2015, located at http://www.christianitytoday.com/news/2015/august/china-sees-red-christian-protest-hundreds-crosses-wen-zhou.html.

In addition, since 2016 the Chinese government has begun to show favoritism toward traditionally Asian religions. In 2016 President Xi Jinping called for greater Sinicization of religion in China, indicating his preference for what is commonly understood as Chinese belief systems—namely Taoism and Confucianism. The president is particularly concerned about Westerners coming to China for religious purposes, fearing "overseas infiltrations via religious means."[18]

Nevertheless, many of China's Christian millions remember the Cultural Revolution (1966–1976), which was disastrous for members of all religions—except for those who had zealous devotion to Chairman Mao and his government. Thus, Christians in China today count their blessings. It could be far worse. Having a cross forcibly removed from the top of the church building is certainly a cause for concern, but at least they are free to worship. They might have to look over their backs from time to time, but there is no doubt that things have changed for the better. And there are good reasons for thinking this trend will continue.

For example, in the city of Changsha, the capital of Hunan province, there is a 260-foot church under construction, already with a large cross crowning its highest point. Notably, the church is twice as tall as China's largest statue of Chairman Mao, which happens to stand only ten miles away. Many have taken notice of this irony, leading

---

18. Quoted in Johnson, "Decapitated Churches in China's Christian Heartland," cited above.

to a public "clash of Christianity and Communism" that has played out on China's social media platforms.[19]

China's relationship with Christianity is significant, and it may be emblematic for virtually all of Asia. As Christianity rises, governments become uneasy, usually because of Christianity's historic association with the Western world. However, as Christianity indigenizes and begins to make helpful contributions to society, this perception could change.

Asia and Missions Opportunities

If I were a missionary, I would turn my face toward Asia. It is a region of the world that is growing in influence, it is opening up to the gospel, and it is a place where Christianity has had little presence before now. In 1900, Asia was only about 1 percent Christian. But Christianity is now blossoming there, and although only a small percentage of Asians are Christian—roughly 10 percent—that number will likely increase in the coming years. We must also keep in mind that we are talking about a region of the world with a vast population, where 10 percent translates to around 400 million Christians.

There are 7.5 billion people on earth, and well over half of them live in Asia. China and India combine for a total of 2.7 billion people—that's over a third of the entire planet's population. Of the world's top ten most-populated nations, Asia

---

19. Didi Kirsten Tatlow, "A Monument to Jesus in the City of Mao," *New York Times*, 7 May 2017, located at https://www.nytimes.com/2017/05/07/world/asia/china-changsha-christian-church-park.html.

claims six: China, India, Indonesia, Pakistan, Bangladesh, and Japan.

Asia is a land teeming with opportunity for Christians. If the faith were to grow in Asia as much as it has in Africa, then it would boost Christianity's numbers to heights never seen before. Christianity has remained at around one-third of the global population for over a century now. In 1910 Christianity could claim about 35 percent of the world's inhabitants; by 2010 it had decreased to around 32 percent.[20] If Asians continue to turn to Christ on a large scale, then Christianity's global numbers could skyrocket in coming decades.

Christianity's growth in Asia is not limited to one region. It is fairly widespread across the continent. Statistically, the most dramatic growth has occurred in the nations of China, Mongolia, Cambodia, and Nepal. We can also point out that Indonesia, Singapore, and Vietnam have in recent years become centers of Christian vitality. Singapore's Christian community increases annually and is now around 20 percent of the population.[21] In Vietnam and Indonesia, Christianity has grown to around 10 percent of the total population in those densely populated countries. While still a minority, it is important to note that the Christian population is growing faster than the overall population growth in these nations.

Cambodia is one particularly encouraging example of a

---

20. See "World Distribution of Christian Population in 1910 and 2010," *Pew Research Center*, 19 December 2011, located at http://www.pewforum.org/2011/12/19/world-distribution-of-christian-population-in-1910-and-2010/.

21. See "Singapore," *Pew-Templeton Global Religious Futures Project*, located at http://www.globalreligiousfutures.org/countries/singapore/religious_demography#/?affiliations_religion_id=0&affiliations_year=2010.

nation poised for Christian growth. During the Khmer Rouge genocide in the 1970s, Christianity was reduced to around two hundred souls. Christian activity was once again allowed in the 1990s, and the faith has experienced powerful growth in the years since. In just the last three or four years, churches have experienced unprecedented signs of openness from the government, allowing them to live without fear. However, as many Christians have warned, that window could close at any minute. Thus, there is a sense of urgency in Cambodia to take advantage of this opportune time. One denomination in particular—the Netherlands-based Christian and Missionary Alliance—has jumped at the opportunity and is making progress.[22]

The Philippines is one Asian nation where Christianity is in the majority, at around 90 percent. With a population of over 100 million, that is lot of people. The vast majority of Filipino Christians are Roman Catholic, stemming from the era of Spanish rule, but the Protestant communities, especially charismatic ones, are on the rise.

There are still some nations and regions in Asia that have shown little response to Christianity, such as Southeast Asia, Japan, Afghanistan, and Pakistan. However, a few of these traditionally non-Christian areas—such as Central Asia—are starting to see modest growth among Christian believers. The Central Asian nations of Kazakhstan, Kyrgyzstan, Uzbekistan, and Turkmenistan are located in a sensitive part of the

22. See Kate Shellnutt, "Cambodians Usher in a Miraculous Moment for Christianity," *Christianity Today*, 19 May 2017, located at http://www.christianitytoday.com/ct/2017/june/cambodians-usher-in-miraculous-moment-for-christianity.html.

world, surrounded by tremendous religious and ethnic diversity: Russians to the north, the Islamic republics of Iran and Afghanistan to the south, and China to the east. Great diversity leads to great sensitivity, and the propagation of faith is often resented.

North Korea is a big question mark. Before the twentieth century, Christianity in what is now North Korea was growing impressively, just like it was in South Korea. The city of Pyongyang—now North Korea's capital—was an important hub for Christian missionary work prior to national division in the 1940s. While Christianity is permitted to some extent in North Korea, it is routinely ranked as the most dangerous nation in the world in which to live as a Christian.[23]

Aspiring missionaries should take note that Asia is the new frontier. There are vast opportunities there for church planting, evangelism, medical missions, and other forms of charitable work. A missionary to Asia could work in the slums of a large city, as did Mother Teresa. She could work among high-tech entrepreneurs in China, South Korea, or Singapore. She could work in rural India among people who need education in everything from birth control to personal hygiene to how to preserve food properly. She could assist with Christian revivals in Indonesia, China, or Nepal. She could plant herself in Southeast Asia and work cross-culturally with Buddhists, or perhaps settle in the vast open

23. See Jeremy Weber, "Worst Year Yet: The Top 50 Countries Where It's Hardest to Be a Christian," *Christianity Today*, 11 January 2017, located at http://www.christianitytoday.com/news/2017/january/top-50-countries-christian-persecution-worldwatch-list.html.

plains of Central Asia and learn how to live dialogically with Muslims.

When we talk about Asia, one thing is certain: China's influence is huge, and growing. Thus, perhaps the most strategic decision a missionary could make would be to learn Mandarin. This one skill will open many doors in a place where countless people are hearing the gospel for the first time, and need their questions answered.

China's rise on the global stage is well known. It is currently expanding its influence to the rest of Asia and Europe through President Xi Jinping's Belt and Road Initiative. This strategy for economic development is supposed to be a resurrection of the old Silk Road so important in world history. However, this time there will be high-speed trains rather than camel caravans. And you can bet that Chinese Christians will be on those trains, and the gospel will expand with them, much like Paul used the Roman roads and waterways two millennia ago.[24]

Asia is rising. And Christianity is rising with it. This is very good news for Christians. And for those who want to get involved, there are boundless opportunities.

The great era of Christian missions is far from over. Now that Asia—with over half the world's population—is encountering Christ, it appears that a new era of missions is barely in its infancy.

24. See Sarah Eekhoff Zylstra, "Made in China: The Next Mass Missionary Movement," *Christianity Today*, 1 January 2016, located at http://www.christianitytoday.com/ct/2016/january-february/made-in-china-next-mass-missionary-movement.html.

7

Coming to America: Asians and Latinos Stake Their Claim

Recently it was my forty-fourth birthday. My lovely wife asked, "What would you like to do for your big day?" I responded, "Let's go visit a church!"

She knows well my passion for exploring churches, and has been a wonderful rock of support for me over the last quarter-century as I've explored Christianity here and abroad. She has accompanied me on many religious-themed trips, so she understood my strange desire. For their birthday, some people might prefer to take a cruise or go to Las Vegas, but I'd rather spend the day with a church that has an interesting story behind it. So it was not a total surprise when I told her I wanted to visit the Mission Ebenezer Family Church in Carson, California.

Carson is only a couple of hours from where we live, so we

loaded the kids into our minivan and made our way toward the east side of L.A.

The Browning of America

When I was a graduate student in the early 2000s at the University of Calgary in Canada, there was a feisty professor who came to our campus to speak, and he had a provocative title for his talk: The Browning of America. He really knew how to pack a room and deliver a powerful presentation. Bringing out the crowds as he did is a fairly rare occurrence in the academic orbit. Even rarer, he lived up to the hype. He cited studies, quoted experts, and projected statistics all to explain how in a short time the United States was going to be majority non-white. It was a fascinating lecture, even though I could tell that his intention was to ruffle a few feathers. The information he presented, however, was not shocking for me. Coming from America's southwest, I grew up witnessing many of the demographic trends he highlighted.

What the speaker didn't mention is that modern notions of racial classifications are completely unscientific categories created in the seventeenth and eighteenth centuries to account for perceived differences in people from various parts of the world.[1] These essentialist and pseudo-scientific theories stereotyped humans by fitting them into fixed categories of

---

1. Johann Friedrich Blumenbach is often thought to be the author of the fivefold division of humans: American Indians, Austronesians, Ethiopians, Caucasians, and Mongoloids. His theories were based on François Bernier's work in the seventeenth century that argued humans are naturally organized into different races based on perceived physical differences.

skin color, perceived differences, behaviors, and other arbitrary generalizations. All of this has been debunked by modern science. Humans are all part of the same single species. Strangely, these obsolete racial and ethnic categories are still commonly used, albeit with profound ambiguity since they have no scientific basis. Still, in defense of the speaker that day, it is nearly impossible to talk about human demographics without some form of ethnic categorization, however insufficient and imprecise.

I grew up in California and New Mexico, where ethnic demographics are commonly discussed due to the rich diversity of these states. New Mexico has long been the standard-bearer state for America's changing demographics. Its population is vibrant, and the state has the highest percentage of Hispanics in the nation, at around 47 percent. Its Caucasian population is around 39 percent.[2]

There are two major reasons for this change: immigration—including undocumented immigration—as well as the fact that Hispanics and Latinos tend to have larger families. Experts predict that the browning of New Mexico is a trend that will continue well into the future.[3] Similar trends are happening across the American southwest, as well as in Florida, Texas, Colorado, and elsewhere.

2. See Jens Krogstad and Mark Lopez, "For three states, share of Hispanic population returns to the past," *Pew Research Center*, 10 June 2014, located at http://www.pewresearch.org/fact-tank/2014/06/10/for-three-states-share-of-hispanic-population-returns-to-the-past/.
3. Melanie Eversley, "Hispanic population swells past white population in N.M.," in *USA Today*, 16 March 2011, located at https://usatoday30.usatoday.com/news/nation/census/2011-03-15-new-mexico-census_N.htm. This article was part of *USA Today*'s coverage of the 2010 census figures.

Currently I live in the megalopolis of Los Angeles—easily America's most populous county—where communities often form around a shared ethnic, cultural, or religious heritage. For example, Tehrangeles, or Little Persia, is an Iranian community. Little Armenia in East Hollywood and Burbank has a large Armenian diaspora population. There are Latino areas such as "Little Havana," African American communities, and several different Asian enclaves such as Indian, Korean, and Southeast Asian. Little Tokyo and Chinatown are important Asian neighborhoods with storied histories. The state of California is extremely diverse, led by its large Hispanic community, which in 2014 surpassed Caucasians as the largest ethnic group in the state.

The university where I live and teach—Pepperdine—reflects the changing demographics of California. For decades our university had a largely Caucasian majority, but that has been changing. In 2016 the Caucasian segment of our student population was down to 48.2 percent.[4]

California is by far America's largest state, and the trends in California look like a harbinger of things to come. For example, the state of Texas is predicted to see a Hispanic majority in the near future. In 2012 Texans were 38 percent Hispanic and 44 percent White.[5]

When I was born in the early 1970s, the Hispanic popu-

---

4. See Pepperdine's fall 2016 student demographics at https://seaver.pepperdine.edu/admission/fast-facts/.

5. Mark Lopez, "In 2014, Latinos will surpass whites as largest racial/ethnic group in California," *Pew Research*, 24 January 2014, located at http://www.pewresearch.org/fact-tank/2014/01/24/in-2014-latinos-will-surpass-whites-as-largest-racialethnic-group-in-california/.

lation was not nearly as large as it is today. For example, in 1970, only one million Mexican migrants lived in the United States. Today, America is home to around 35 million Hispanics of Mexican origin, or, around 11 percent of the U.S. population. About a third of all Latinos in the U.S. were born in Mexico, a relocation of people that has been labeled "one of the largest mass migrations in modern history."[6]

Indeed, by the year 2044 no single ethnic group will hold a majority in the United States. Recently, NPR put it this way: "The country is changing—it's getting browner." They based their projections on the fact that White growth is slowing down. An example can be found in America's kindergartens, where non-whites are now in the majority.[7]

Another example is the decline of Whites in 53 percent of America's 3,100 counties in the first decade of the twenty-first century. New York City and Los Angeles have each lost over a million White people since 1990. Fewer than half of America's babies born since 2011 are Caucasians.[8]

Asians, Africans, and Caribbean peoples are knocking at America's door as well. For example, the birth tourism phenomenon attracts many Asians because America is one of the few nations that automatically confer citizenship on people

6. Ana Gonzalez-Barrera and Mark Lopez, "A Demographic Portrait of Mexican-Origin Hispanics in the United States," *Pew Research*, 1 May 2013, located at http://www.pewhispanic.org/2013/05/01/a-demographic-portrait-of-mexican-origin-hispanics-in-the-united-states/.

7. Domenico Montanaro, "How the Browning of America Is Upending Both Political Parties," *NPR*, 12 October 2016, located at http://www.npr.org/2016/10/12/497529936/how-the-browning-of-america-is-upending-both-political-parties.

8. See Christopher Caldwell, "The Browning of America," *Claremont Institute*, 9 March 2015, located at http://www.claremont.org/crb/article/the-browning-of-america/.

who are born on its soil. Many Chinese people believe the greatest gift they could ever give their child is American citizenship. As a result, a birth tourism industry has developed in several American cities, most prominently in Los Angeles. These families don't necessarily relocate to the United States, but eventually, they want to offer their children the great opportunities that America provides, especially when it comes to a university education.[9]

The year 2016 was unprecedented for immigrants entering the U.S.[10] The number of immigrants who passed into California was up by 500 percent from the previous year. And more than a third of those people are not even from Latin America. Many come from Haiti. But we are seeing an increasing number of Asians: Indians, Chinese, Nepalese, Bangladeshis, and Pakistanis. These people often sell everything just to get to Mexico—a stone's throw from the promised land. But when they arrive, they are often detained in Tijuana or Mexicali, and languish for months in holding centers. Their families back home helped them finance a trip that can cost them $10,000 in hopes that by anchoring themselves in the U.S. they can eventually sponsor more members of the family.[11] For some of them, persistence pays off and they manage to get into the U.S. Others are turned away and

9. See Frank Shyong, "Why birth tourism from China persists even as U.S. officials crack down," *L.A. Times*, 30 December 2016, located at http://www.latimes.com/local/lanow/la-me-ln-birth-tourism-persists-20161220-story.html.
10. See Alexandra Zavis, "Haitians, Africans, Asians," *L.A. Times*, 22 December 2016, located at http://www.latimes.com/projects/la-fg-immigration-trek-america-tijuana.
11. Zavis, "Haitians, Africans, Asians."

must decide whether they can manage the long journey back to their home country without sufficient resources.

Large numbers of Chinese, Filipino, Indian, Vietnamese, and Korean immigrants have made their home in America. Today there are around twenty million Asian Americans in the U.S., many of whom are foreign born. According to a major study on Asian Americans by Pew Research, those who manage to get into the United States tend to adjust well to their adopted nation. In fact, three-fourths of Asian American adults were born outside the U.S. They tend to speak English well, value education, work hard, and have comparatively high incomes. Asian American households average $66,000 in annual income as opposed to the rest of the nation's average of $50,000. For a group that constitutes only about 5 percent of America's population, Asians are particularly adept at gaining admission into premier universities, where they tend to major in lucrative fields. Taken as a whole, Asians are the wealthiest, best-educated ethnic group in the U.S. today. Perhaps more importantly, they are the fastest-growing.[12]

Mission Ebenezer Family Church

The whole point of our birthday weekend trip to Carson was to attend a church I had heard good things about: the Mission Ebenezer Family Church. Founded in 1959 by Miguel and his wife Lupe Canales, the church is a member of the Assemblies of God, a large Pentecostal denomination. Over

12. See the summary report, "The Rise of Asian Americans," *Pew Research*, 2012, located at http://www.pewsocialtrends.org/asianamericans-graphics/.

the years, the church relocated a total of seven times, sometimes meeting in the pastor's backyard.[13]

In 1980, Miguel and Lupe's son Isaac took over as senior pastor, along with his wife, Ritha. It was during Isaac's tenure that the church experienced dramatic growth. Isaac is a fascinating and gifted person, with excellent credentials: a BA in Religion from Vanguard, an MDiv from Harvard Divinity School, and a PhD in New Testament from Fuller Theological Seminary. It was during Isaac's leadership that Mission Ebenezer came to be known as one of the most important Hispanic churches in Los Angeles.

In 1959 Mission Ebenezer began with fifteen people. Today, the membership is around 3,000 strong, with five worship services each Sunday in both English and Spanish.

I first heard about this church through one of my colleagues, Dan Rodriguez. He wrote a book on Latino Christianity that I reviewed for a journal. In that book he referenced Mission Ebenezer. When I stopped by his office one day to tell him I planned to go observe the church, he told me about the Canales family and how impressive they are, not just as church ministers, but as genuinely good people.

The Canales boys are gifted, and not just in a pastoral sense. For a time Josh, the eldest, was a professional baseball player and even earned a short stint with the Dodgers. He's a gifted preacher, but his greatest strengths are in his ability

---

13. See the church's website at http://www.missionebenezer.org/about. I also gathered information on its history during an interview with Josh Canales, one of the current pastors and son of the current senior pastor, on 23 April 2017, on location at Mission Ebenezer. I am very grateful for his willingness to welcome us and have a nice long visit.

to connect well with the members of the congregation. The congregation respects him. He invests tremendous time and energy in the church, and it is clear that he is deeply loved and appreciated. Josh married a Nigerian woman, and they have been blessed with a family. As a result of their marriage, a good-sized Nigerian community now worships there.

Everybody at Mission Ebenezer knows Josh is the future senior pastor of the church, but his two brothers are deeply respected there as well. The second son, David, is a quarterback and receiving coach for the Seattle Seahawks, but he partners with the church in a variety of ways and preaches when he comes to town during the off-season. The third son, Coba, is a gifted preacher who also serves as a pastor at Mission Ebenezer. He was in the pulpit the Sunday my family and I visited, and delivered a powerful message. The boys and their dad all rotate on Sundays, sharing the preaching load so that no one gets overwhelmed.

Mission Ebenezer consists of seven buildings on 5.5 acres. When we pulled up to the property, we noticed security guards checking cars and allowing people into the parking lot. We had already gathered that this was a tough part of town, but this was the first church I had ever visited with a security detail.

Immediately upon entering, what I noticed about this congregation is that it is extremely diverse, a tone set by Pastor Isaac who is Hispanic while his wife is from Dutch ancestry. When you enter the church it quickly becomes clear that this congregation is committed to the radical inclusion of the gospel. Rich or poor, Black or White, tattooed or not, people from all backgrounds call this church home. This diversity is refreshing, especially given the famous observation by Martin Luther King Jr. that 11:00 a.m. on Sunday morning is the most segregated hour in America. That statement does not ring true at Mission Ebenezer, however. The crowd was thoroughly mixed: Black, Brown, Asian, White, all worshiping together.

Ethnically, Mission Ebenezer is a fairly accurate microcosm of Los Angeles. This diversity has come at a cost, however. Pastor Josh admitted, "If we wanted to go brown, this church would be at 10,000." He explained to me that most people are more comfortable with their own ethnic group, but the Canales family feels that God has called them to cross all ethnic and racial lines in their ministry, not only because of the context of Los Angeles, but because of the gospel itself, which for two thousand years has firmly rejected the notion of ethnic division.

This church is a reflection of the local community, too. When Pastor Josh brought me into the sanctuary, he shook hands with everyone with such love and joy to see each person there. It was clear that he had built relationships with these people over the course of many years. He shook hands with and embraced many of the young men who were there. The service I attended was a relatively young crowd; many of the attendees had tattoos and piercings.

At one point Pastor Josh whispered into my ear saying, "See that guy over there? He just got out of prison on Friday.

This is his first Sunday out. He became a Christian through our prison ministry."

Many of the members at Ebenezer have overcome serious obstacles and challenges in their lives. Many of them had little background in the Christian faith until after they were grown. By following Christ, some had to make a radical departure from their former lifestyle.

I found it fascinating that this church has a large building on the campus geared to help people stay off the street—an excellent weight gym, pool tables, exercise machines, and—notably—two boxing rings. Young men come into their church from the L.A. gang culture, whether Black, Hispanic, Samoan, White, or Asian. Some of them were even members of rival gangs, but have come to realize that fellowship in Christ trumps all of their previous commitments. Some of these people have never channeled their anger in constructive directions. So they are provided with a room full of hanging sandbags. Boxing teaches them how to control their temper and stay within themselves. This church understands life in the inner city, and knows how to serve those populations quite well.

Mission Ebenezer is an inspiring place to worship because of its wonderful sense of inclusion, warmth, and gracious hospitality. It is a mosaic and melting pot of ethnicity, income level, and age. Among their twenty-one pastors, four are Caucasian, one is Asian, four are African American, and the rest are either Hispanic or ethnically mixed. In our interview, Josh acknowledged that the church is openly accepting to all, regardless of country of origin or ethnic affiliation. His perspective was refreshing for me to hear, and so obviously in line with the teachings of the gospel that these identity markers should not divide those who are in Christ. Mission Ebenezer takes pride in its diversity without making a big deal of it. It is diverse and everyone is welcome, and everyone knows that.

When challenges arise, the church deals with them head on. Pastor Josh discussed how sometimes when racial tensions—whether national or local—are in the news, Mission Ebenezer preaches sermons unequivocally condemning human-made divisions. And his approach is to emphasize the radical inclusivity of the gospel, which requires that people love one another, deeply, and without regard to skin, hair, or eye color. Christian love goes beyond tolerance. It is a love that goes from one person's heart to another's. It is much more radical than simply tolerating differences in the people around you. In fact, Pastor Josh said, "We don't like the word 'tolerance.' Tolerance is a word you use when you don't like the other person. We believe in a full kingdom embrace." I emphasize the word "embrace" here. Having grown up in a world where people hug each other frequently, I felt right at home at Mission Ebenezer.

Pastor Josh said America is browning, and there will always be a major pipeline connecting the U.S. to Mexico, whether you build walls or close all the tunnels or restrict immigration. You can hide your head in the sand or you can embrace the flow of people coming from Latin America. Clearly, the

Canales family has decided to dive in and contribute to the multiethnic context of L.A. rather than retreat from it. It is an opportunity to witness to the gospel.

I asked Pastor Josh about theology, and what they preach in such a diverse setting. He said, "We pride ourselves on preaching God's word. We preach Christ." He emphasized the authority of the Bible, but with tremendous love toward every single person who comes. He said there are times when people get upset at the gospel and perhaps even walk out during a sermon. But, he said, the gospel is often uncomfortable, and they've actually lost people through the years because of their biblical commitments. However, the far more common scenario is that lives are changed, and the hatred and anger begin to melt away in the presence of Jesus. The way of the world is no longer attractive when the gospel takes root in someone's heart.

At one point I asked Pastor Josh about their denominational affiliations, if any. He responded quickly, and boldly: "We're Pentecostal. We don't try to be Presbyterian or Methodist. We are fully Pentecostal." Pastor Josh emphasized that Pentecostalism is a gift, an aspect of their church background that should not be hidden. He is fully aware that some people are uncomfortable with charismatic forms of faith, but, in his words, "We've experienced Pentecostal fire here, and the Holy Spirit has restored lives."

As we were leaving, Pastor Josh took us back to the auditorium, pointed to the pianist and said, "See the guy on the piano? He's been playing music here for forty years." Then he went back to his hugs and handshakes with the members, calling each of them by name, smiling, embracing the kids, and personally encouraging every single person who came within fifteen feet. I thought to myself, "That right there is an effective pastor."

Berean Community Church

Thirty miles down the road, just off the 405, is the town of Irvine, an affluent city in the white-collar community of Orange County. A number of high-tech corporations are headquartered there, and the residents tend to be highly educated. I visited the Berean Community Church there to witness yet another expression of American Christianity.

Our visit to Berean began rather painfully. When we pulled into the parking lot, my eight-year old daughter accidentally got her hand slammed in the large sliding door of our minivan, causing us to consider a trip to the emergency room. Right away we were approached by some people who wanted to help us out. They sent for a woman who works professionally as a nurse. When the nurse arrived, she gave us ice and bandages and consoled my daughter. After the bleeding and crying simmered down, we brought her with us into the auditorium instead of checking her into the children's program with our other three kids. She fell asleep almost immediately on my wife's lap out of sheer exhaustion due to the traumatic experience. (When she awoke, she was fine.)

Berean Community Church is almost completely Asian. More specifically, it is an *East* Asian church, comprised of mostly Koreans and Chinese, with a few Vietnamese, Filipino, and Japanese. They are well educated and highly motivated. They take careful notes on the sermon and engage in a variety of fellowship opportunities geared to help them navigate through life effectively alongside their Asian brothers and sisters in the congregation.

Berean began as a Baptist church, but soon experienced a split. The group that split off was mainly young people in their twenties. They established themselves as an independent church in 1997, and for about seven years remained at around thirty to forty members. Life was difficult for the pastor, Peter Kim. He sold his house to finance the ministry. He was very close to giving up when a young man from the University of California-Irvine started attending regularly and asked Pastor Kim to mentor him. That young man is now the associate pastor of this church. His name is Mark Lim, and I interviewed him in person during the visit and then by phone the following week.[14]

The church is quite young, a reflection of their relatively youthful leadership. Pastor Mark is thirty-five years old, and Pastor Kim is forty-eight. They are the only paid pastors at Berean, though the congregation benefits from the service of a host of people who step up as volunteers.

Just a few years ago, the church actually had six pastors on the payroll. In 2014, one of them—Aaron Choi—was sent to northern California with a group of families for the purpose of planting a church there. It was a successful endeavor,

14. My interview with Pastor Mark Lim took place on 4 June 2017.

and that church now has 180 members. Another pastor was sent to do missions in China. Another transitioned to become a staff member of Compassion International. And another joined the secular workforce.

The first thing my wife and I noticed once we settled into our seats for worship was that we were the eldest in the room of about five hundred. Nearly every chair was full, and it seemed like a youth gathering for college people and young professionals. I asked Pastor Mark about this, thinking perhaps we had attended a college service. But he confirmed that it is simply a young church. I asked him if they target young people, and he said not specifically. They began as a youthful bunch, and have maintained that vibe. Now they have many young families. My wife and I had never seen a cry room—visible through a large window in the back—so full. Pastor Mark said only about thirty of their members are above age forty. The majority of them are between twenty-five and thirty-five. They have around 110 college students each Sunday, mostly students at the University of California at Irvine.

Pastor Mark said that they don't really have a target group when it comes to age. However, they do try to target men. "We want to give a lot of attention to the fathers. We focus on fathers, so they will be a stronghold for the church with their maturity and consistency." Berean has a vibrant and extensive ministry to families. Focus groups meet regularly and discuss helpful books such as a current one by Francis Chan, an Asian American pastor in California who is a leading voice in the American evangelical scene.

This noticeably youthful church surprised me with their worship style. There was no pizazz, no impressive lights, and no particularly attractive performances attempting to win over young people who might otherwise be tempted to check their phones. Rather, the sermon was relatively straightforward—not full of jokes or illustrations to keep people's attention. Instead, it was a rather serious exhortation on how to work hard like Paul, to stay focused on Christ, and to allow Christ to live in us.

One theme that Pastor Mark returned to repeatedly was that true discipleship requires discipline and hard work. Using Colossians 1:24–29 as his text, he argued that we, like the apostle Paul, should contend strenuously in our faith, with divine energy provided by Christ.

At several points during the hour-long sermon, Pastor Mark referenced parents. He candidly discussed the stereotype of Asians pushing their kids so hard, and he strongly affirmed this approach to parenting. He told a personal story of his parents emigrating to the U.S. from China. His parents often reminded him, "We've worked without vacations so that you will have opportunities." Pastor Mark's parents came to America knowing absolutely no one. He emphasized how hard he watched his parents work in those early years. He encouraged the parents in the congregation to be firm yet patient with their children in order to guarantee the child's success.

Throughout the sermon, Pastor Mark urged the members to struggle for Christ, struggle for higher and higher

standards, and work hard to live up to the high expectations
set by self-sacrificing parents. Toward the end of the sermon
he declared,

> God is not okay with just coasting. God wants us to
> strive for more. Christ has higher standards. Stop making
> excuses. God can transform us. We are enabled by God
> to achieve perfection. Christ can perfect all of us, Amen?
> We need to struggle and work hard!

In a candid moment during the sermon, Pastor Mark said he
has been rebuked in the past for working too hard. However,
he said, the apostle Paul teaches us that we *should* work hard.
He claimed he would never retire from pastoring because his
goal in life is to work harder and contribute more to God's
kingdom.

In the sermon's conclusion, Pastor Mark began to speak to
the members like a father would speak to his son or daughter. He urged the members to stop making excuses, especially
considering the fact that their parents had sacrificed everything for them. Additionally, Christ gave up himself, and the
apostle Paul sacrificed his own comforts for the sake of the
gospel. In loving but stern words, he told the people that it is
misguided to think we should take it easy in our faith. Rather
we should always be willing to sacrifice more for the gospel.

At one point in the sermon Pastor Mark discussed Millennials, saying their parents had sacrificed all for them, yet many
of them preferred to take it easy in life. But, he warned, to
cave in to the temptation to be lax was the absolutely wrong

decision. He urged the Millennials in his congregation not to squander their opportunities—opportunities their immigrant parents never had. Rather, they should make good use of these valuable opportunities that their hardworking parents earned through blood, sweat, and tears. As he noted in my interview with him, "You hand people life on a platter and they take it for granted."

I asked Pastor Mark, "Why are Asian Americans so ambitious?" In his view, it is due to the honor/shame dichotomy in their culture. He stated, "You must continue to advance to honor your family and yourself. This is ingrained into Asians when they are young." He remarked that his parents are economically comfortable now, but they still save everything in ziplock bags because of the extremely lean years, both in China and in their early years in America. He then stated, "You will rarely see a homeless Asian." However, he admitted, the Millennials' generation of Asian Americans are showing many of the same traits of other Americans: "They want to be treated like adults, but they haven't earned it." He said the most effective method to combat this sense of entitlement is through Christian discipleship.

Pastor Mark is one who backs up his preaching with actions. He works hard to contribute to the Asian community in Irvine, which accounts for around half of the city's population of nearly 300,000 people. Not only does he pastor the Millennial-heavy Berean Community Church, but he also spends every Wednesday on the campus of U.C.-Irvine. He is a highly motivated, extraordinarily disciplined man, and he works hard to make a difference in his community. And he is optimistic that Christianity will continue to grow in the Asian community in Irvine as well as in the United States. He cited other nearby Asian churches that are making a difference, such as Gospel Life Mission Church in Anaheim and Living Hope Community Church in Brea. Each has 150 college students in their churches and is poised for rapid growth when those young people start having families.

It was clear to me that Pastor Mark has an optimistic view of Asian Christians in America. And his optimism is justified when you look at some of the recent research into the faith of Asian Americans. Some scholars, for example, have discovered a striking trend when it comes to Asian immigrants into the United States: they tend to become Christians once they arrive on our shores. Sociologist Jerry Park discovered that "44 percent of all Asian-Americans are Christian."[15] That is a remarkable statistic, given the fact that, globally, Asians are only about 10 percent Christian. And it is young Asians who are turning to Christianity most often.

I asked Pastor Mark about the future of his church there in Irvine. I mentioned to him that it must be bright, considering the fact that the cry room was so full during the worship service. He chuckled and admitted that, indeed, his church was beginning to experience a major baby boom since most of the congregants are in the fertile years of life. He's not worried about the rapid growth on the horizon, however. They are

15. Jerry Park's research is cited in Wesley Granberg-Michaelson, *From Times Square to Timbuktu* (Grand Rapids, MI: Eerdmans, 2013), 89.

well prepared. He assured me that they could keep up, saying: "We have over thirty volunteers in the nursery."

Christ the Destroyer of Barriers

Between the years 2008 and 2015, I pastored a church in Pasadena that consisted mainly of African Americans. It was an enriching experience for me and my family, and I hope for the church. In countless ways I was blessed by these sisters and brothers in Christ who became like family for my family and me.

During my time with them, I came to realize the great diversity of the members. African Americans are every bit as diverse as White Americans, and skin color is only one of several aspects of a Black person's identity. We had wealthy members and struggling members. One man had great success as an engineer for Chevron. Another spent several decades as a public school administrator. One spent time in prison, but is back on track and now has two beautiful daughters with his wife who is also a member. One elderly gentleman served honorably in the U.S. military for many years. Another is a successful businessman from Panama who emigrated to the U.S. as a boy. One younger fellow works as an emergency room cleanup technician; he and I like to get our families together and attend Dodger games.

The African American women are equally diverse. Two of them are nurses. One works as a beautician. One works at a legal firm. One is a security officer and has to come to church in uniform because she gets off the job directly before worship services. One woman held a desk job for the city administration for many years but is now retired; she is known as G-ma and loves to provide her amazing home cooking for our monthly potlucks. One was an actress and is proud of her membership in SAG (Screen Actors Guild). One taught elementary school for many years but recently retired. One works at a grocery store. One young lady works for a nanny company.

While there is tremendous diversity in the membership, there are also some things that unite the African American members. Politically they tend to be Democrats, although on certain issues they are quite conservative. And while they are all proud of Obama, they also had misgivings about a few of his policies when he was in office. It is a fact that African Americans tend to vote Democrat; however, they don't just write a blank check to the Democratic Party. They have their criticisms of their party just like most people do.

One Sunday after the 2008 U.S. presidential election, I noticed an African American gentleman in the lobby with his face in his hands. He was shaking his head as if to be saying "no." I sat down next to him and asked, "John, what's going on, brother?" He responded, "I just cannot believe this nation elected a Black president." I told him that it was not a huge surprise considering the advanced polling results. He then looked at me and clarified, "Dyron, I was raised in Mississippi in the 1960s. Yes, I saw the polls, but I did not think it would or could actually happen."

That moment will be locked in my mind for the rest of my

life. And while I will probably never understand the power of that election for an African American person, I will never forget the impact that it made on John. President Obama made Black Americans very, very proud. And whether people support the Democratic Party or not, all Americans should respect the great dignity and affirmation African Americans felt when he was elected to the highest office in the land.

And one day when an Asian or Latino president is elected, we must extend similar respect. These are milestones. As Christians, we must rejoice with them that rejoice because their dignity and identity are affirmed during those historic moments. We are the body of Christ, where there is neither Jew nor Greek, slave nor free, male nor female. In Christ we are one, and we affirm the dignity of one another as if it was our own dignity being affirmed.

What I learned about my African American sisters and brothers in the congregation is that once they realize you love them, respect them, and can be trusted, they will open their hearts to you. As I look back, I may have sensed a little caution in them when I was first hired to be their minister. But that vanished quickly when it was clear I was there to serve them, and to be the best pastor that I could be for them. In return, they covered my family in love. They taught my kids in Sunday school, cooked meals for us, celebrated with us when we had a new baby, and treated us with deep kindness and sincere affection. They, too, saw how much my family and I respected them and wanted to be part of their lives. When I visited them in their homes or in the hospital, or counseled with them, or had them into my home for a party, they knew I was on their team and that I loved them with the love that comes from being one in Christ.

The members came to accept me, my teachings from the pulpit, and even my perspectives on potentially divisive topics. For example, one African American woman in the church fell in love with a Caucasian man. Initially her family had issues with the arrangement whereas his family was fine with it. We worked through some of these issues together during pre-marital counseling and eventually everything worked out fine. I was asked to perform their wedding and they now have a wonderful, stable marriage that enjoys the strong support of both families.

I am fully aware that my experience was unique and special. I consider it a great privilege that I was able to witness firsthand how Christ can destroy barriers that often separate people. I am reminded of the problems that persisted in the early church between Jews and Gentiles. There was suspicion and caution. They struggled to understand each other's worldview. But the power of the gospel enabled them to get through those struggles, and eventually the two became one, and God was glorified by their efforts.

Over the course of centuries, the Christian church has crossed many borders, and continues to cross borders, whether political, ethnic, economic, or national. As the gospel helps us to realize our profound unity in Christ, I believe my family's experience in a largely African American church is a beacon of hope.

I am proud of the fact that for several years my three older children were rooted in an ethnically diverse community of faith. All they knew was that their church consisted of people who had dark skin and hair, in contrast to their own light skin and hair.

My twins—who are now aged ten—are already fairly outspoken about their beliefs that it doesn't matter whether people have light hair or dark hair, or blue or brown or green eyes, or light skin or dark skin, or come from different places. These are ideas that we discuss relatively often. Because of their upbringing and experiences in the mainly African American church I served, my children have come to believe it is ridiculous for people to mistreat each other based on differences in skin and hair color. They argue that it would be like treating someone poorly because they happened to be wearing a dark blue jacket rather than a light blue one—or something just as arbitrary.

Sometimes in my research I wonder whether it is harmful to split people into groups by race and ethnicity for the purpose of understanding what is happening in the world of Christianity. In this chapter, I have separated out Latinos, Asians, and African Americans for the sake of understanding Christianity in America. But it is far wiser to take the biblical example for how to understand differences in peoples. In Ephesians 2:14–22, Paul acknowledges that there are distinct differences between Jews and Gentiles, but when they are in Christ, they are completely reconciled:

For he [Christ] himself is our peace, who has made the
two groups one and has destroyed the barrier, the divid-
ing wall of hostility. . . . His purpose was to create
in himself one new humanity . . . thus making peace
. . . and in one body to reconcile both of them to God
through the cross, by which he put to death their hostility. . . . Consequently, you are no longer foreigners and
strangers, but fellow citizens with God's people and also
members of his household, built on the foundation of the
apostles and prophets, with Christ Jesus himself as the
chief cornerstone. In him the whole building is joined
together and rises to become a holy temple in the Lord.
And in him you too are being built together to become
a dwelling in which God lives by his Spirit.[16]

The United States of America has a wonderful opportunity
to build churches that reflect this profoundly inclusive vision.
We err if we allow divisions over race, ethnicity, or class
to erode our fellowship in the Spirit. We are all being built
together in the name of Christ.

America is becoming more diverse, but the gospel stands
in judgment of us if we privilege one shade of skin over any
other. In Christ, we are joined together, as a holy temple, so
that Christ can take residence within. And as Christ rose from
the dead, we too will rise up together. Indeed as Christians
we already are rising up together. And this is the most exciting reality of global Christianity. As we rise, God comes near.

16. New International Version.

8

America's Role: To Be Good Soil

Like many American Christians, I grew up in a rural setting, where church was at the center of communal life. My little church was the Southside Church of Christ. And I was very fortunate to have grown up in it because it was a church with very good soil.

By that I don't mean the church was built on good farmland; I mean this church was receptive, nourishing, and fruitful. My home church there in Portales, New Mexico, is still doing the wonderful work it did when I was growing up. From its inception, it has served as the home church for the New Mexico Christian Children's Home, and its ministries revolve around helping orphans and getting families back on their feet. They've broadened their work to include a substantial single mothers' ministry. On the church grounds they built apartment complexes for struggling families, unwed mothers, and others living in distress. This is the kind of congregation that I believe Jesus envisioned: they care most about service to the poor and suffering. Still today I stand in awe of the enormous good this church has accomplished over the decades.

This church has very good soil. Its receptivity to those in need is exemplary: broken families, orphaned children, and immigrants. New Mexico is a state with very high immigration rates from Latin America. And those immigrants often have basic needs that go unmet for months or even years. Perhaps only part of the family is in the U.S. legally, and thus they are separated. Or perhaps the parents have to work so hard that they are unable to invest fully in the lives of their children, especially if their work requires them to be gone for weeks at a time. Or perhaps they simply don't earn enough money to make a living, and thus find themselves without enough food, or without regular healthcare.

Small-town immigrants rarely draw attention to themselves or their plight because they realize this kind of attention could get them sent back to their home countries that they tried to leave. So they quietly work, and they quietly persevere, realizing that although America is not necessarily the land of plenty for themselves, their children just might enjoy its benefits one day.

I didn't realize it at the time, but the church I grew up in was doing precisely what Jesus asked them to do: they were being good soil.

Parable of the Sower

The Parable of the Sower in Matthew 13 is one of the most powerful stories that Jesus told.[1] It is not necessarily among the most famous of his teachings, but it is important for Christians to understand its nuances.

The parable is about a farmer who goes out to sow seeds. He's tossing the seeds here and there and they land in places both good and bad. Some seeds fall onto the path where he is walking, and the birds come along and eat them. Some seeds fall onto rocky ground where there is not enough soil, so they are unable to take root. Some seeds fall into the thorny bushes, where they get choked out. But some seeds fall where they are supposed to fall—on good soil. And those seeds produce massive crops, "a hundred, sixty, or thirty times what was sown" (v. 8).

The disciples did not quite understand what Jesus was trying to teach, so he interpreted it for them. He said some people hear the word of God but don't fully understand what they are hearing, so the devil takes the opportunity to snatch away the teachings. Some people hear the gospel and rejoice, but they don't develop deep roots in the faith. So they fall away whenever any turbulence comes along in their life. Others hear the gospel but get tempted by worry and by wealth, choking them to the point that they are unfruitful. There are always some, however, who hear the word of the

---

1. The Parable of the Sower is also found in Mark 4 and Luke 8.

Lord and come to understand it well. Those are the ones who thrive, and produce extraordinary amounts of fruit.

Throughout my life and ministry, I have found this parable to be clarifying and helpful. Many people hear about Christ, but for whatever reason they don't feel compelled to join the Christian faith. This has been the case with many church plants, mission endeavors, and evangelistic campaigns. Missionaries have sailed halfway around the world to share the good news, only to come up empty in terms of converts. Many domestic church planters have moved across the country with high hopes that they will plant a church that will thrive, only to become discouraged and eventually abandon the project. That's the downside of the parable, but it is often true.

However, the good news of the parable is that sometimes the gospel takes hold. And when it does, you can expect to see an abundant harvest. This is precisely what happened in Africa, some of the best soil that missionaries could have ever imagined. In Asia, Korea was good soil. The Philippines also proved to be excellent soil, especially for the Catholic missionaries who worked there. The Pacific Islands are another place where the gospel took root; they are almost thoroughly Christianized today.

Now, however, Western people tend not to sign up for a lifetime of missionary service like they did in previous generations—for many reasons. For one thing, it is a different world today, politically speaking. Western nations cannot simply plant their flag on an island and claim it for Spain or

England. Today there are international laws that cannot be violated, and national autonomy must be respected. Missionaries are unwelcome in many nations today. In other places, it makes little sense for an American to travel to do mission work because the place is already Christianized.

There are still many among us, however, who desire to sow the seed of the gospel. What, then, should they do since they cannot necessarily become a pioneering missionary to a foreign land? I think the answer is clear: Christians should become the "good soil" that Jesus described. We should welcome those who come to our shores—whether Christian or not—and show them the love of Christ in hope that they will come to understand the message of Jesus more clearly through our hospitality.

And furthermore, when non-Westerners turn to Christ, they enrich our faith. They bring experiences that we ourselves have not had. They see Christ in a very different way than we do, especially if they come from a place of crushing oppression, or desperate poverty, or chaos and war. When Asians, Africans, Latin Americans, or Eastern Europeans enter our communities, they diversify and enrich them. It is very similar to the idea that when you travel you learn more about yourself and your own culture. When we encounter difference in our communities here in the U.S., we will undoubtedly reflect anew on ourselves.

It is easy to forget that early Christianity was a Jewish religion. One ethnicity. Jesus was a Jew, as were all of his apostles. But when gentiles joined the faith, Christianity blossomed magnificently. Just as the God of Abraham, Isaac, and Jacob has become the God of so many nations, the gospel of Christ is also at a pivotal, even epochal moment in human history. It has gone global. And a global gospel is far preferable to a limited, ethnic, geographically bound gospel. Christians should welcome these developments and embrace them. God is doing something new by bringing in people from all nations, tribes, and languages.

Just as at Pentecost, God's message is expanding to reach all people. And as Christians we need to either facilitate that global encounter, or get out of the way. I am reminded of Acts 5, where a teacher of the Jewish law began to consider whether God was opening up to new peoples. The text warns that if God was indeed using Christ's followers for divine purposes, then it was foolish to oppose them. For if their teachings are from God, "You will not be able to stop them; you will only find yourselves fighting against God" (v. 39).

Opportunities Are Right Next to You

Misión Pan de la Vida (Bread of Life Mission) is a small gathering in Passaic, New Jersey, that began when St. John's Lutheran Church decided they wanted to reach out to the community around them. They made big plans to cook breakfast for the poor and disenfranchised in their community. They advertised extensively, with good intentions of showing neighbors their serious desire to serve them, like Jesus did. The plan seemed well conceived. The only caveat was that if you wanted to enjoy a hot and tasty breakfast, you were expected to come to church on Sunday, and immediately following services everyone would enjoy food together. Problem was, nobody came. Not one.

After what seemed like a failed initiative, one man in the congregation spoke up. He said he often drives by Home Depot and notices there are always a few dozen men from Latin America standing around, waiting for someone to hire them for an hour or two doing hard labor. They just might enjoy a hot breakfast.

It is a common sight in so many of the large cities in America. These men can make better wages doing sporadic day labor in the U.S. than they could ever earn in their home countries. So they stand on the street corner in the cold, awaiting someone to motion to them and offer them something to do, whether painting a fence, cutting down a tree, or installing a bathroom sink.

The members of the congregation liked the man's suggestion and decided to take all the food down to Home Depot, where it was welcomed with open arms. The workers greatly appreciated the hot breakfast. When the members at St. John's offered to bring breakfast the following Sunday, the men enthusiastically agreed. That was five years ago, and the ministry continues, with around fifty workers enjoying the breakfast weekly.

What began as a breakfast has morphed into a short church service. The pastor of St. John's began offering word and sacrament right there in the parking lot for the hungry immigrant men. Now the services are led in Spanish by the workers themselves. One of them reads a scripture and another distributes communion. Although "most of them didn't go past elementary school," there is always someone who will step up to read.[2]

The ministry to the Home Depot workers became a satellite congregation to St. John's. Members now treasure the opportunity to partake in the body and blood of Christ with these migrant workers who are far away from home. A good relationship has developed, and the workers welcome the smiling parishioners each Sunday.

The pastor of St. John's—a young man from Chile named Rev. Ignaki Unzaga—is a graduate of culinary school with a passion for feeding the hungry. Combining his talents, he spearheaded this initiative to provide sustenance for the soul and food for the body to the men gathered at Home Depot.[3]

In an interview, Pastor Unzaga encouraged others to look for ways to change the church from where you are planted in the world. With so many people coming to the United States, mission work can often be done from wherever you are, if you have the eyes to see and the ears to hear what is happening around you. Unzaga said, "It's about where you are, knowing who lives among you and learning how you can be in relationship with those people. Opportunities are right next to you."[4]

2. See Megan Brandsrud, "The face of the church is changing," *Living Lutheran*, December 2016, 16–17.
3. For information on Rev. Unzaga, see http://www.goodshepherdglenrock.org/meet-our-staff.html.
4. Brandsrud, "The face of the church is changing," 18.

Misión Pan de la Vida sprang out of a context where a church was simply trying to be good soil. In the beginning the parishioners felt like they could offer a hot meal to hungry workers, but in the end, the table turned. The congregation benefited from the encounter every bit as much as the immigrants did. Both were enriched. And not only were the workers blessed with food, but they were also empowered by the dignity of leading a worship service of their own, in their own language. The recipients of grace began to bestow grace. And that is a huge lesson for all of us. When we give, we receive. Just as Jesus promised, "Give, and it will be given to you. A good measure, pressed down, shaken together and running over, will be poured into your lap. For with the measure you use, it will be measured to you" (Luke 6:38).

As Pastor Unzaga said, the opportunities are always right there. It just depends on how we handle them. If we, in the American church, handle this situation well—as did St. John's—we are sure to bless others, and, in turn, we will be blessed in myriad ways as well. This is a key part of being good soil. By allowing good fruit to grow in our land, we too are able to enjoy the abundant harvest.

One issue that goes unaddressed in the Parable of the Sower is *how to become* good soil. Even the best soil has to be tilled, softened, de-weeded, and watered in order to become productive. Even very hard ground can become soft and fertile if given the chance. In becoming good soil, we might have to remove a lot of weeds and extract several stones, but eventually that ground will become receptive to the seed.

And as Christianity changes, and as the world changes, Christians in America need to spend some time preparing the soil. Our fruitfulness depends on our willingness to prepare.

Immigration Is Good for Christianity

Immigration has been a critical part of the Christian story from early on. Not only is immigration a key part of many Old Testament stories such as those of Abraham and Moses, but it is also an important part of the gospel.

Deuteronomy 10:18–19 reads, "The Lord defends the cause of the fatherless and the widow, and loves the foreigner residing among you, giving them food and clothing. And you are to love those who are foreigners, for you yourselves were foreigners in Egypt." In Deuteronomy 26:12 the Lord commands the Israelites to set aside a tenth of their harvest in order to help the priests, the foreigners, the fatherless, and the widows. Deuteronomy 1:16 urges the Israelite community to give a fair hearing to foreigners, just as they would to members of their own nation. Deuteronomy 24:14 commands Israelites to pay foreigners a fair wage, rather than exploiting them. In Jeremiah 7:6, God instructs his people not to oppress the foreigner, the fatherless, or the widow. In the Old Testament, the foreigner—the immigrant—is among the most vulnerable, deserving of protection and care.

Similarly, the New Testament is explicit about how immigrants should be treated. In one important passage about the judgment day, Jesus associates care for the immigrant with salvation: "I was hungry and you gave me something to eat,

I was thirsty and you gave me something to drink, I was a stranger and you invited me in, I needed clothes and you clothed me" (Matthew 25:35–36). The apostle Paul pointedly advises Christians to "practice hospitality" (Romans 12:13). A very interesting passage on immigrants occurs in Hebrews 13:2, where the author writes, "Do not forget to show hospitality to strangers, for by so doing some people have shown hospitality to angels without knowing it."

Fundamentally, the gospel is a story of immigration—Jesus comes to earth to save humankind and direct them toward God. In addition, Jesus and his family lived as migrants for a period of time during the persecution of baby boys under King Herod the Great. Joseph moved his family to Egypt after being warned in a dream that Herod wanted Jesus killed. This situation is not altogether different from the experiences of so many people throughout the world today who are trying desperately to escape persecution, war, poverty, or the hopelessness that comes from living in a failed state.

Immigration to the United States provides Christians with opportunities to practice what they preach. Whether a citizen agrees with current government policy on immigration is beside the point. It is the obligation of every Christian to provide help and care to the person in need, and that person is often an immigrant. Christians are not commanded how to vote on these issues, but we are commanded how to deal with those who enter our towns and cities. We are expected to treat them with the same dignity that we want for ourselves, as Jesus says, "Do unto others as you would have them do unto you" (Luke 6:31). According to Jesus in Matthew 25:34, our salvation is connected to our response to foreigners: "Come, you who are blessed by my Father; take your inheritance, the kingdom prepared for you since the creation of the world."

In all these ways, immigration is good for Christianity. We are provided an opportunity to be good soil—to serve God, and to provide care for others. We are forced to overcome our prejudices. We are put in a position where we help those who can scarcely help us in return. In looking after the immigrant, we recognize that our citizenship is in heaven (Philippians 3:20), rather than within an arbitrary boundary line drawn on the earth. Immigrants are human beings, created in the image of God. They are not first and foremost citizens of Mexico, Guatemala, or Pakistan. They are beloved creations of the same God who called us into existence. They deserve the right to flourish in life just as we have. And by being good soil, we help them to begin their journey toward independence, safety, and prosperity, just as we were given similar opportunities by those around us.

Immigration is good for Christianity in other ways, too. It is a natural way by which we can grow the church. The vast majority of Latinos who come into the United States are Christians. And when they come into the U.S. they will likely connect themselves to a church if that church is willing to invest in them. This is how faith communities multiply. People find a body of believers who share their convictions, and if they are welcomed, then they pledge their commitment or their membership to the church.

When we speak about immigration in America, we enter into a fraught political discussion. As Christians, however, we must recognize the difference between faith and politics. Christians can, and do, have differing views on immigration and border policy, but we are all called to nurture those vulnerable immigrants who happen to make it into the United States. There is no conflict here. Doing the work of Christ is a responsibility that supersedes our national citizenship. Loyalty to Christ surpasses any other loyalty, whether local, national, or even denominational. Christ urges us to look after the immigrant. Therefore we must feed the itinerant worker. We must provide shelter for the Salvadoran family. We must invite the Somalian refugee in so that they can be cared for.

Of course when we welcome immigrants, a terrorist may also slip into the U.S. There may be immigrants who become dependent on public assistance, especially in the early phases of their arrival. Some women may enter the United States strictly in order to gain American citizenship for their baby. Some immigrants will commit crimes. Alas, these are all realities that do affect us, sometimes personally.

However, there is another side to all of these scenarios. Many of these people will integrate, will join our society, will become members of our churches, and will remember how someone welcomed them—in the name of Christ. Jesus said, "Let your light shine before others, that they may see your good deeds and glorify your Father in heaven" (Matthew 5:16). Some of these immigrants will notice this light shining inside of us, and will be drawn to it. And eventually they will give glory to God, perhaps even while standing next to us during worship on a Sunday morning.

For centuries America has been good soil for the immigrant, and the U.S. will likely continue to be one of the top destinations for them. Every one of us who is privileged to live in the United States has a history. We, too, descend from immigrant families. Our ancestors—whether from Angola, Ireland, or Germany—came here and struggled to make it. And thank God for the people who lived as good soil, and accepted the immigrants into their communities, towns, and cities.

Some of our ancestors came here under terrible conditions—enslaved, escaping deadly famine, or evading capture from a tyrannical regime. The same is true today. Many immigrants come to this country under unthinkable circumstances. Like our ancestors, they are willing to risk their lives to enter the United States, whether legally or illegally. Once they get here, we need to remember our own story. We also should remember the word of the Lord to the Israelites, "Do not mistreat or oppress a foreigner, for you were foreigners" (Exodus 22:21).

A New Kind of Missionary

Reverse missions is a concept that has gained attention in recent years. Basically this is the idea that while Americans and Europeans used to relocate to Africa, Asia, and Latin America to spend a life in missionary service, the tables have turned. American Christians still practice missions, but typically they return home after a week or two. On the other hand, when foreigners come to the Western world, they tend to stay. These are a new kind of missionary.

Missionaries these days are often migrants. They come to the United States to study in our universities or to escape chaos in their own nations. Some of them simply come here to start a new life, much as my ancestors did when they came from Ireland and Scotland. They felt they could achieve much more in America, so they sold their possessions, made the journey here, and never looked back.

I can relate to this scenario somewhat. I became a kind of missionary in 1999 when I moved from Texas to Canada so I could pursue my dream of earning a PhD and perhaps eventually teaching in a university. My wife sold her Chevy Corsica, and we packed our possessions into a small U-Haul trailer, and headed to Calgary, Alberta, where I had been accepted into the university. Our first year was difficult. We lived in a small basement suite owned by some people we met in a local church. My wife was a nanny for a Korean couple. I graded papers for a professor. We managed to survive, but there was great stress wondering how we would possibly get ourselves out of this compressed situation.

Help came all at once. My wife was cleared by the government to teach and was offered an elementary position at a Mennonite school. I was called to part-time ministry in a small church of thirty to forty people. Quite suddenly we were in a position of teaching and preaching, my wife in a school and me in a church. This is the new kind of missionary service. You move to a new land, and a welcoming Christian community surrounds you with love and hospitality, and gives you an opportunity to serve. For us, we had climbed up life's ladder by several rungs. Instead of eating pasta, bread, and cereal all the time, after gaining better employment we were able to shop for meat, fresh fruits, and vegetables.

Canada was good soil for us. My wife's school gave her a dependable salary. The church welcomed us with open arms and paid me a livable wage. They treated us with dignity, giving us sick leave and time off for vacation. The government of Canada was also gracious to us. They allowed us to use their healthcare system. Our twins were born in 2006. It was a very difficult, high-risk pregnancy for my wife, but we did not have to worry about our financial liability. The people of Canada footed our medical bills through the paying of their taxes. Of course we paid into the socialized healthcare system, too, but I am sure that in this case the care that we were given was worth much more than what we paid.

In 2011–2012, my family experienced the hospitality of another nation—this time it was Argentina. We traveled there to lead my current university's year-long study-abroad program. And although we were not planning to live there beyond the academic year, we were treated like citizens. The Argentine government allowed our three children to attend public school for free.

We also relied on the services of the socialized healthcare system in Argentina. I broke my wrist while playing soccer and was treated by a doctor who spoke almost no English. Drawing from my limited Spanish and his limited English, I was able to determine that the emergency room doctor's father had attended university at "Heorya Tesh" many years before. It took me a few minutes to realize he was actually trying to pronounce "Georgia Tech," but with his heavy Spanish accent it was difficult to understand.

I suspect my doctor's father relied on Americans when he was in the U.S. And there I was, an American, depending on his son many years later. Not only did I rely on the services of the doctor, I also relied on the benevolence and good will of the Argentine nation, for I did not have to pay for that trip to the medical clinic that night. He reset my wrist and carefully applied a cast—that ran from my fingertips to my armpit—for free. I was grateful that my nation had proven itself hospitable to this man's father at some point in the past when he was being educated at Georgia Tech. I became the beneficiary of hospitality flowing back in the opposite direction.

What many Americans don't realize is that Latino immigrants to the United States are often looked after by Latinos who are already here. It is far more likely for a Spanish-speaking immigrant to connect with a Spanish-speaking community. Latino American churches bear a much greater burden than others when it comes to looking after immigrants from Central and South America. These churches are not loaded with resources, either. They are typically quite small in their membership, consisting of people mainly from the working class. It is normal for these congregations to move every few years, especially in California where the rent is astronomically high.[5]

In most cases, these middle-class churches still have close connections to their home countries in Latin America, so they send a good portion of their offerings to charitable works there, whether a church plant, orphanage, or elder-care home. They realize that by earning money in the U.S. they are far better off than most of the people back home. So they scrape together whatever benevolence they can and wire it to their home countries through Western Union.

This is the current state of missions. It is much more com-plicated than the nineteenth-century template of wealthy nations sending missionaries to poor nations. Today, mission work is from everywhere to everywhere. And no longer can we say that mission work is for the rich. Fuller professor Juan Martinez states, "Poor Christians around the world never got the memo that you needed money to do missions."[6]

However, when all of those blue-collar migrants pool their money together, it can be a sizeable sum indeed. It is esti-mated that migrants to the United States send well over $100 billion abroad each year, with Mexico being the largest ben-eficiary. That far exceeds the American government's con-tribution of $33 billion, and the private sector's $44 billion.[7]

---

5. For a helpful article, see Andy Olsen, "The Migrant Missionaries," *Christianity Today*, July/August 2017, 39–48.
6. Olsen, "The Migrant Missionaries," 43.
7. These statistics come from Olsen, "The Migrant Missionaries," 42. See also Nurith Aizenman, "Mexicans in the U.S. Are Sending Home More Money Than Ever,"

Immigrants in the United States are making a huge impact on many lives abroad. They have the connections, they understand the needs, and they are able to work more efficiently due to their closeness to the culture.

It might come as a surprise to learn that not only does the U.S. send out the most missionaries, but it also *receives* the most missionaries.[8] There are over 30,000 foreign missionaries working in the United States.[9] Many Christians worldwide see the United States as a place in need of the gospel. For instance, the Brazilian-based Universal Church of the Kingdom of God has planted nearly two hundred churches in the United States.[10]

As America continues to diversify, we are seeing an increasing number of foreign missionaries to the U.S. As international connections are made, financial and religious flows will increase in both directions. Mexicans who settle in the U.S. will send money to Mexico and will do mission trips to Mexico. Korean Americans who settle in the United States will establish close relationships with their sending congregations in Korea. Nigerian denominations that are planting

NPR, 10 February 2017, located at http://www.npr.org/sections/goatsandsoda/2017/02/10/514172676/mexicans-in-the-u-s-are-sending-home-more-money-than-ever. Pew Research has a helpful chart that breaks down global remittances, although it should be kept in mind that there is room for error since not all remittances are tracked. See "Remittance Flows Worldwide in 2015," *Pew Research Center*, 31 August 2016, located at http://www.pewglobal.org/interactives/remittance-map/.

8. See "Faith on the Move," *Pew Research*, 8 March 2012, located at http://www.pewforum.org/2012/03/08/religious-migration-exec/.

9. Robert Wuthnow, *Boundless Faith: The Global Outreach of American Churches* (Los Angeles: University of California Press, 2009), 56.

10. Todd Hartch, *The Rebirth of Latin American Christianity* (Oxford: Oxford University Press, 2014), 189–90.

churches here will use funds raised in the U.S. to strengthen their denominations back in Nigeria. People living in diaspora remain conscious of their home country, and establish larger, more nuanced networks. It is a reciprocal process that strengthens Christianity everywhere.

Migration to the United States is making an impact on the religious tapestry of our nation, and sometimes the effects of this process show up in surprising places. For instance, Asians, especially Koreans, account for a good percentage of the evangelicals in America's most prestigious schools. Researcher Rebecca Kim provides the following snapshots:

- 80 percent of evangelicals at University of California Los Angeles and University of California Berkeley are Asian American.

- 70 percent of Harvard Radcliffe Christian Fellowship's members are Asians.

- Yale's Campus Crusade for Christ chapter is 90 percent Asian. Twenty years ago it was 100 percent White.

- At Stanford, InterVarsity Christian Fellowship is nearly entirely Asian.

- Over the last fifteen years, InterVarsity Christian Fellowship saw its Asian American numbers grow by 267 percent.[11]

As the West continues to diversify ethnically, there is no

11. Rebecca Kim, *God's New Whiz Kids? Korean American Evangelicals on Campus* (New York: New York University Press, 2006), 1–2.

doubt that these zealous evangelicals with roots in Asia will make a lasting impact on the religious terrain of American universities and cities, and, ultimately, the nation's culture.

Being Good Soil

It is a fascinating statistic that 40 percent of Asian Americans are Christian, especially when you learn that, globally, Asians are only about 10 percent Christian.[12] In other words, when Asians move to America, many of them convert to Christianity. I suspect that one common reason they become Christians is because of what they see in the Christians they encounter. Like many immigrants to America, they come here needing significant help. They want to raise their kids in a healthy environment. They crave a social network. And they end up turning to the churches—usually Asian American ones—that accept them and offer support. Those Asian American churches have become good soil for other Asians who come this way.

While national immigration policy is extremely complicated, Christian teaching is not. We help them. We feed them. We find them medical treatment. We offer them a place to stay. If they become incarcerated, we visit them. By doing these things we show ourselves to be good soil. We are also fulfilling the commands of our Lord.

Becoming good soil requires sacrifice, but for Christians,

---

12. See Wesley Grandberg-Michaelson, *From Times Square to Timbuktu* (Grand Rapids, MI: Eerdmans, 2013), 89. See also Dyron Daughrity, *Church History* (New York: Peter Lang, 2012), 234–38.

the benefits are substantial. People will turn to Christ when they see our good deeds, when they feel our love, and when they experience the nonjudgmental grace that we are able to provide.

Christians in America have massive opportunities to spread their faith throughout the world, and they can do it by staying at home and being good soil to the immigrants who come this way. Each year, about 1.5 million people immigrate legally to the U.S. Recently, India and China overtook Mexico on the list of nations sending the most immigrants to the U.S.[13] And the vast majority of Indians and Chinese are not Christians. These people will require help, and it would be ideal for churches to step up to help them. If Christians want to reach people with the gospel of Christ, then we must not miss this incredible opportunity to witness our faith to the tens of thousands of people who are coming directly to our cities, towns, and neighborhoods.

Today, there are nearly 50 million legal immigrants living in the United States. But this is nothing new. We have always been a nation of people descended from immigrants. For good reason, the U.S. is known as a melting pot, a united people who have come from extremely diverse backgrounds. Or, as our national motto states, *e pluribus unum* (out of many, one).

For Christianity to continue to thrive in America, it will

13. See "Frequently Requested Statistics on Immigrants and Immigration in the United States," *Migration Policy Institute*, 8 March 2017, located at http://www.migrationpolicy.org/article/frequently-requested-statistics-immigrants-and-immigration-united-states.

require American Christians to be that good soil that Jesus describes in the parable of the sower. We must do our part to help these people get on their feet. If churches want to appeal to these people, then they would be wise to help them in their time of need—help them transition smoothly into this nation. Jesus said, "Truly I tell you, whatever you did for one of the least of these brothers and sisters of mine, you did for me."

Let us not prove ourselves to be bad soil: rejecting people, preventing them from thriving, allowing them to languish in prison without justice, watching them suffer with no access to healthcare. That would be cruel. And no one wants to join a faith that conducts itself in this way.

Rather, the way of Jesus, the good soil approach, is to serve those around us, especially the immigrant. They are extremely vulnerable without assistance.

By welcoming others, whether Christian or not, we contribute to Christianity's rise. As Christians, we are at our best when we come to the aid of those who need it. And when these people witness our love and genuine care for them, they will take notice. If they join us, we become that much stronger, and that much more diverse. And the cycle will continue. We bring people to Christ, who bring people to Christ, who bring people to Christ. And in this way Christ is glorified. And Christianity continues to rise, yielding a crop that is thirty, sixty, or a hundred times what was sown.

9

Christianity Is Changing...
and It's Worth Celebrating

"It's like Disneyland!" Those were the words of Mande Mae, my eight-year-old daughter, when we first stepped onto the campus of Saddleback Church, in Lake Forest, California.[1] Saddleback is one of many American churches defying the claim that Christianity is dying, and after having visited, I can say that without a doubt it is not. Rather, Christianity is *rising* in a big way. Yes, even in a place like southern California, known more for its secularity than for its religiosity.

My wife and I meandered into the large, multilevel children's building to check our four little ones into their classes. We stopped to take a look at the aquarium. My kids suddenly ascended the rock-climbing wall. The greeters welcomed us, serving our kids ice-cream sundaes as they headed toward the upbeat music in their classrooms. Even our two-year-old

---

1. Our family attended Saddleback Church on Saturday evening, 3 June 2017.

darted off to class. My wife and I looked at each other. "Well, no problem dropping them off!"

Everyone we passed smiled and said hello. People ordered burgers and fries or Chick-fil-A at the outdoor cafés nearby, while an excellent live band played "Let It Be" by the Beatles. Teenagers sat in the grass, listening to the music, enjoying themselves, in no hurry to make it on time to the upcoming church service. The sermon was to be delivered by Rick Warren—one of America's most celebrated pastors, known for *The Purpose Driven Life: What on Earth Am I Here For?*—a book that has been called "the bestselling hardback non-fiction book in history," as well as "the second most-translated book in the world, after the Bible."[2]

Saddleback is very different from what I am used to in a church. I've always worshiped in small churches, where there were never enough volunteers, always a dearth of resources, just two or three staff members, and a humble facility. Saddleback, however, is like an outdoor shopping mall, a theme park, and a concert all wrapped into one. It is a church that has its finger on the pulse of American Christianity. Churches that thrive are churches that understand the needs of their members. And Saddleback meets those needs with top-notch children's facilities, computer systems for keeping track of kids, a beautiful campus, plenty of parking, relevant music, tasteful and contemporary décor, dozens of service oppor-

2. These claims are from the publisher Zondervan, located at http://www.zondervan.com/the-purpose-driven-life. No one seems to know for sure how many copies of this book have been sold, but estimates are in the tens of millions. Zondervan claims it has been translated into more than eighty-five different languages.

tunities, well-organized small groups, various food options, professional staff, and more.

At the beginning of the service, I sort of expected an extrovert emcee to jump up on stage and say "Hello! I can't hear you! Hellooooo!!! How is everybody doing out there?" But that is not what we got. Rather, a man calmly took the stage and asked us to pray. Before we prayed, however, he said, "I realize that for many of you, today was a bad day. So take a deep breath. Be comfortable. You can calm down. We're a family." I took a deep breath and bowed my head, knowing that in a room of that size there were surely some who needed to hear those words.

Saddleback is quite informal, with plenty of the California stereotypes: flip flops, sundresses, shades, and muscle shirts. But it is also relevant to its cultural context. Like its southern California setting, it is racially diverse, with a welcoming aura about it. It is a church where you connect to the body of Christ *as you are*.

Pastor Warren's message dealt with how a life with Christ should be a grateful and generous life. God created us, and he wants to be with us. He wants to help us with our daily challenges. He is on our side. Warren's parting advice was: "Stop complaining. Be grateful. Your days will improve dramatically if you start the day being grateful. Don't be a cynic, doubter, and critic. Don't live your life that way."

Saddleback's approach to Christianity resonates with Americans. Their smorgasbord of ministries meets the spiritual and emotional needs of its people. But it is not a church that is strictly self-serving. They are also engaged with the wider world.

For example, Saddleback's partnership with the government of Rwanda in the aftermath of the genocide is an amazing example of how to bring hope to others. The church's Peace Plan equips their members for short-term missions: from educating youth in Africa, to bringing disaster relief, to fighting sex trafficking, to medical ministry. It is no wonder that so many Californians have found Saddleback to be a place where they can connect, serve, and grow in their Christian walk.

And that is the beauty of Christianity. When it is done well, it excels in its relevance, equipping people for service in the kingdom of God. Just as Christianity is a story about a God who came to earth and assimilated to our culture, Christ's followers are at their best when they assimilate to the cultures they interact with. Globally, Christianity is reaching people all over because of its ability to connect effectively with various cultures. In the last century or so, Christianity has accomplished this feat with amazing results.

Saddleback's steady rise is just one of many examples we could point to that demonstrate just how vibrant Christianity in America is today. But that is only a small snapshot of what is happening globally. From Asia to Africa to Latin America to Europe, Christianity continues to defy the premature forecasts of its demise.

The Death of Christianity Was Greatly Exaggerated

On 8 April 1966, *Time* magazine featured an ominous-looking, black-and-red cover that asked, "Is God Dead?" Today, however, if *Time* magazine featured a cover story on Christianity, it might read: "The death of Christianity was greatly exaggerated."

No, God did not die. And Christianity is not a relic of the past. It is very much alive. And while the future of the Christian faith seems to be anchored in the global south, there are many examples in the West—Saddleback is one of them—where Christianity is not only surviving, but thriving. It is reinventing itself. It is connecting with people in the twenty-first century as well as it has in any century before. The future of Christianity is bright, and when we in the Western world take a more global view, we realize it is blossoming in places we've hardly ever associated with the faith.

For example, in China, we are witnessing today the rise of a potential Christian powerhouse. People are turning to Christ there in numbers that we've rarely seen in history. And people in influential positions—politicians, businessmen, professors—are quietly spreading their faith, and showing people around them how Christianity and China are perfectly compatible. Sociologist of religion Rodney Stark argues that if the Chinese Christian community continues at its current annual growth rate of 7 percent, there could be nearly 600 million Christians in China by 2040.[3]

---

3. Carl Bunderson, "Why is Christianity growing so quickly in mainland China?," *Catholic News Agency*, 17 August 2015, located at http://www.catholic-

India—known historically as the graveyard of missionaries—is seeing spectacular Christian growth. The city of Hyderabad—a technology powerhouse—is home to the world's second-largest congregation—Calvary Temple. The church began in 2005 but today has over 150,000 members. And it has not even started to plateau in its membership, since 80,000 of them have joined only since 2013. The founding pastor, Satish Kumar—with ties to Rick Warren—claims half of his membership is under thirty years old, and the vast majority of them are from non-Christian backgrounds.[4]

The Russian Orthodox Church is enjoying a new wave of religious vitality as they carry out a massive project of church construction. In Moscow alone there are two hundred new churches under construction to accommodate the millions of members in the city.[5] One mammoth-sized church dedicated to the victims of Soviet persecution has been erected on the site of the Sretensky Monastery with the proceeds of a wildly popular Russian book called *Everyday Saints and Other Stories*. This bestseller highlights exemplary Russian Orthodox Christians who stood firm in the faith during years of hostility. It has sold millions of copies, bringing in tremendous revenue for the church.[6] The Russian Orthodox building project

newsagency.com/news/why-is-christianity-growing-so-quickly-in-mainland-china-57545/.

4. Jeremy Weber, "Incredible Indian Christianity: A Special Report on the World's Most Vibrant Christward Movement," *Christianity Today*, 21 October 2016, located at http://www.christianitytoday.com/ct/2016/november/incredible-india-christianity-special-report-christward-mov.html?start=2.

5. Anna Vasilieva, "200 new Orthodox churches in Moscow causes public stir," *Russia Beyond the Headlines*, 26 March 2013, located at https://www.rbth.com/society/2013/03/26/200_new_orthodox_churches_in_moscow_causes_public_stir_24285.html.

is not limited to Russia, either. For example, it recently built a massive cathedral and cultural center in Paris very close to the Eiffel Tower.[7]

Christianity's worldwide growth has caused some interesting institutional developments in historically Western denominations as well. For example, the Assemblies of God, a Pentecostal denomination begun in America in 1914, now has far more members overseas. One of its churches, the famous Hillsong Church in Sydney, Australia, has over 100,000 weekly worshipers through its powerful music and media ministry.[8] Singapore has two Assembly of God congregations with memberships in the thousands—Grace Assembly of God and Trinity Christian Center. New Life Assembly of God in Chennai, India, is home to 40,000 members.[9] Calvary Church in the majority-Muslim nation of Malaysia has seven thousand members.[10] The largest church in the world—Yoido Full Gospel Church in South Korea—is an Assemblies of God congregation boasting 800,000 members.

Another interesting development is the Anglican Church. Today, there are far more Anglicans in Africa than in

6. Paul Kaiser, "Gigantic, Super-Ornate New Church Built by Monks to Open Soon Next to KGB in Moscow," *Russia Insider*, 4 December 2016, located at http://russia-insider.com/en/politics/moscow-prepares-honour-new-martyrs-and-confessors-new-church/ri17780.

7. Tom Heneghan, "New Russian Orthodox cathedral in Paris reflects Moscow's growing global role," *National Catholic Reporter*, 21 December 2016, located at https://www.ncronline.org/news/world/new-russian-orthodox-cathedral-paris-reflects-moscows-growing-global-role.

8. See the church website fact sheet located at https://hillsong.com/media/.

9. Warren Bird, "Global Megachurches," located at http://leadnet.org/world/.

10. Bird, "Global Megachurches."

England. That trend is sure to increase, as well, since Anglicanism is declining in Britain, but continues to grow steadily in Africa.[11]

The Roman Catholic Church—the largest denomination in the world—is also shifting to the global south. Only about 24 percent of Catholics are located in Europe today. Latin America is the epicenter of the church, with 39 percent of its global membership, and the home of its current pope. But the most dynamic growth has been in Africa (16 percent) where Christianity has grown dramatically over the last century. Today, the top three nations with the largest Catholic populations are Brazil, Mexico, and the Philippines. The nation with some of the most remarkable signs of growth, however, is the Democratic Republic of the Congo—a nation of over 80 million people that is around half-Catholic.[12]

Nigeria is home to many megachurches, and ten of them have memberships in excess of ten thousand. In the city of Lagos you can stand just about anywhere, throw a stone, and hit a megachurch. Winner's Chapel has 50,000 members. Redeemed Christian Church of God also has 50,000. Apostolic Church has 40,000. Lord's Chosen Charismatic Revival Church has 30,000. Christ Embassy also claims 30,000. Daystar Christian Centre has 25,000 members. Mountain of Fire and Miracles claims 20,000. T. B. Joshua's Synagogue

11. "Global Anglicanism at a Crossroads," *Pew Research Center*, 19 June 2008, located at http://www.pewforum.org/2008/06/19/global-anglicanism-at-a-crossroads/.
12. "The Global Catholic Population," *Pew Research Center*, 13 February 2013, located at http://www.pewforum.org/2013/02/13/the-global-catholic-population/.

Church of All Nations claims 15,000.[13] And these are all just in the city of Lagos!

The story of Christianity is not just a story of growth, however. It is also a story of how our faith meets real needs all across the world. As Christianity encounters global cultures—often for the first time—it is making an impact. Many of these cultures are finding Christianity to be a supportive ally, helping them to deal with problems, to improve the lives of their people, and to provide hope.

In Kenya, senior Christian clergy have taken the leading role in preparing the public for free and fair democratic elections. This is crucial work, because in 2007–2008 the nation was rocked with violence in the aftermath of an election that left hundreds killed and hundreds of thousands displaced.[14]

Meeting in Malawi, young Christians from sixteen African nations recently participated in an Eco-School on Water, Food, Health, and Climate Justice to think through the implications of climate change, and how it impacts the African continent. In many African nations, the church is the best hope for mobilizing people for social transformation. Participants pooled their efforts together after hearing the challenges of many regions on the African continent. And together as Christians, they are figuring out ways to solve catastrophic

---

13. See Warren Bird, "Global Megachurches—World's Largest Churches," located at https://docs.google.com/spreadsheets/d/1YIKShcapvO6LatV5WG7P4XXczuoaw9 EAfKv3IMJwXnQ/edit?hl=en_US&hl=en_US#gid=0.

14. See "Ahead of Kenya elections, concerns about peace emerge," *World Council of Churches*, 3 August 2017, located at https://www.oikoumene.org/en/press-centre/news/ahead-of-kenya-elections-concerns-about-peace-emerge.

problems such as drought, famine, and illnesses that come from dehydration and water pollution.[15]

Recently in Jerusalem, Middle Eastern Christians advocated for nonviolent solutions to the Israel-Palestine conflict by joining Muslims for prayer inside the Al Aqsa Mosque. Though a small community in Israel and Palestine, Christians are an influential one, and they serve an important intermediary role between Muslims and Jews. Christians in Jerusalem serve a critical role advocating for peace—the way of Jesus—in an extremely volatile context where violence can erupt suddenly.[16]

In Cambodia, the minority Christian community has played a major role in decreasing sex trafficking through the Christian human rights group IJM (International Justice Mission). The organization's top lawyer in the country is Sek Saroeun, a convert to Christianity. Sek and his team worked with Cambodia's anti-trafficking police to rescue hundreds of sex slaves and prosecute many of the ringleaders in court. Other Christian groups like Agape International Missions have transformed the brothels into churches, clinics, and factories to provide employment for those leaving the sex industry.[17]

15. See "African youth takes stand at first ever WCC Eco-School," *World Council of Churches*, 3 August 2017, located at https://www.oikoumene.org/en/press-centre/news/at-the-intersection-of-climate-change-water-food-and-health-youth-take-a-stand-for-africa2019s-future.

16. See "Muslims and Christians pray together for just peace in Al Aqsa Mosque," *World Council of Churches*, 28 July 2017, located at https://www.oikoumene.org/en/press-centre/news/muslim-and-christians-pray-together-for-just-peace-in-al-aqsa-mosque.

17. Kate Shellnutt, "Cambodia's Child Sex Industry Is Dwindling—and They Have

In the midst of the Russian-Ukrainian conflict, Christian missionaries on the border are holding prayer rallies, providing firewood, and helping to feed people affected by the violence. One pastor, Sergey Kosyak, has opened the Bread of Life bakery in Maryinka with the help of Mission Eurasia. His bakery gives away five hundred loaves each day for free, along with Bibles. With bombshells exploding nearby, these Christians realize that war often causes people to search for meaning. And they try to provide that meaning—found in Jesus Christ—despite the daily menace of errant mortar bombs.[18]

It is encouraging to see so many people all over the world not just converting to Christ, but serving others in his name. Western Christians have much to learn from our sisters and brothers in dangerous contexts and truly impoverished places as they work hard to make Christ manifest in extremely challenging settings, whether in Jerusalem or Rwanda or eastern Ukraine. These Christians are unsung heroes. But when we realize the sacrifices they endure for the sake of the gospel, perhaps it will cause us in the West—usually with comfortable lives—to rethink what it means to be a Christian.

Many Christians in the world must think long and hard

Christians to Thank," *Christianity Today*, 19 May 2017, located at http://www.christianitytoday.com/ct/2017/june/cambodias-child-sex-industry-trafficking-christians.html.

18. See Andrew Kramer, "In Ukraine Towns Ravaged by War, Evangelical Missionaries Find Fertile Ground," *New York Times*, 3 March 2016, located at https://www.nytimes.com/2016/03/04/world/europe/in-ukraine-towns-ravaged-by-war-missionaries-find-fertile-ground.html. See also "Daily Bread and Bombs in Ukraine," *Christianity Today*, 20 May 2016, located at http://www.christianitytoday.com/ct/2016/june/daily-bread-and-bombs-ukraine.html.

about whether to practice their faith because it could potentially imperil their lives or the lives of those close to them. Daily, Christians suffer for the faith, and some are even killed for their commitment to Christ. Most of their stories remain virtually unknown in the West, but a few manage to reach our newspapers, such as the seemingly endless rounds of violence against Coptic Christians in Egypt over the last several years. Or the four nuns running a nursing home in Yemen who were killed by the Islamic State in 2016.[19] Or Guinean pastor Moise Mamy and his eight-member medical team who were killed in cold blood in 2014 while trying to fight Ebola in remote villages.[20] Or the Chinese Protestant pastor Rev. Han Chung-ryeol, who was murdered with an axe in April 2016 due to his work among North Korean exiles and refugees.[21] These stories should inspire us and make us aware that for some, Christianity is a precious treasure, guarded deep within.

But Christianity was born in persecution. The apostle Paul, too, realized the preciousness of the Christian faith, especially under persecution, when he wrote:

19. Mary Chastain, "Yemen's Missionaries of Charity: The Nuns Killed by Islamic State Jihadists," *Catholic News Agency*, 8 March 2016, located at http://www.catholic-newsagency.com/news/here-are-the-faces-of-the-nuns-who-were-martyred-in-yemen-84893/.
20. Abby Phillip, "The fear and hopelessness behind the deadly attack on Ebola workers in Guinea," *Washington Post*, 19 September 2014, located at https://www.wash-ingtonpost.com/news/to-your-health/wp/2014/09/19/the-fear-and-hopelessness-behind-the-deadly-attack-on-ebola-workers-in-guinea/?utm_term=.d619406046 55.
21. "Protestant clergyman who helped North Koreans axed to death in China," *AsiaNews.it*, 5 May 2016, located at http://www.asianews.it/news-en/Protestant-clergyman-who-helped-North-Koreans-axed-to-death-in-China-37410.html.

We have this treasure in jars of clay to show that this all-surpassing power is from God and not from us. We are hard pressed on every side, but not crushed; perplexed, but not in despair; persecuted, but not abandoned; struck down, but not destroyed. We always carry around in our body the death of Jesus, so that the life of Jesus may also be revealed in our body. For we who are alive are always being given over to death for Jesus' sake, so that his life may also be revealed in our mortal body. So then, death is at work in us, but life is at work in you. (2 Corinthians 4:7–12)

Paul realized something very few of us in the West have to face. In our sufferings, Christ is revealed. And when someone dies for Christ, their precious faith is sure to rise up in the lives of others.

Changes Are Happening

Over the last generation or so, many Western Christians have been persuaded to believe that Christianity is dying. And from a certain narrow perspective, that did indeed appear to be the case. But while "Christianity may have been pronounced to be at death's door . . . it's firmly back in the public space."[22] It was never dead. In fact, as we've recounted throughout, it is thriving.

Time magazine's "Is God Dead?" cover caused alarm

---

22. "Jesus Is Alive in London," *Christianity Today*, 24 April 2016, located at http://www.christianitytoday.com/ct/2016/may/jesus-is-alive-in-london.html.

among Christians, particularly about the future of our faith. But when we take a closer look at Christianity on a global scale, I think it is safe to say God is not dead, and neither is the church. When Jesus established the church he announced to Peter that not even the gates of hell could prevail against it (Matthew 16:18). Indeed, Christianity is here to stay. And just when it appeared it was losing steam in the West, it surged to new heights in surprising places around the globe.

By no means is Christianity finished in America or in Europe either. Rather, it is changing. The old ways of practicing the faith are being cast aside in favor of new ways, and Christians should be happy with the developments. Changes are not only welcome, but necessary if we want our faith to thrive in the twenty-first century and beyond.

Christians in the West are anxious about the future of the church. And I suppose that is normal. Lifelong Christians are proud of the church; they worked hard to build it. And it is not easy to see so many changes in such a short period of time.

The beauty of global Christianity, however, is that we now witness the fruits of those Christians' labors: their mission work, their benevolence, and their commitment to teaching Christ to future generations. All of that effort is paying off today as we witness Christianity's astonishing global rise.

Our world is changing dramatically, so it makes sense that the church changes with it. To try to remain in the past is to take the path of irrelevance. Young people don't want to sing songs written by people many generations ago. They want to write their own songs, and reinvent Christianity afresh for their own generation. It is our duty to equip them in the same way that we ourselves were equipped.

Furthermore, we Christians must be aware of the changing demographics of our nation, and the implications these developments have for the church. People long to come to the United States, and we have an amazing opportunity to share our faith with them.

But when we accept people into our midst, we should not expect them to be passive or silent. They become full members, equal to us, and they will bring their own perspectives into our churches. New perspectives bring change. But that is the beauty of global Christianity. We expand individually as our faith expands collectively. Our faith is a great gift to the world, and people are accepting it with gratitude, and embracing it with open arms. And it is our responsibility to rejoice with them in their salvation. They have discovered the gift that a life with Christ brings. Now they are crafting their own Christian identities, which will not be exactly like ours.

New members in a church always bring new gifts. When immigrants join our churches, they will have much to teach us, much to share with us, and much to offer us. But we won't be able to receive them if we withhold our hospitality from them. By welcoming them we open ourselves to being shaped by them. However, in return, by joining with us, they too show they are willing to be shaped by us.

It is a mutually beneficial encounter that has been occurring within the Christian faith ever since Paul took the gospel to the gentiles. And we should remember that Paul's actions did not come without controversy. Looking back, however, we realize it was the right thing to do. God called Paul specifically for this task. And the result was that Christianity crossed many boundaries when it morphed from a Jewish, ethnic faith to a faith for all people everywhere. So many more people have experienced the power of the good news because of that transcultural encounter.

It should be exciting to think of immigrants to America as being potential partners in the gospel with us. Christianity's tendency to be ethnocentric and segregated won't hold much longer. Unstoppable changes are happening all over the United States. Immigrants, refugees, and international students are now a constant presence in our cities, from San Francisco to Denver to Albuquerque to Houston to Atlanta to New York. Chicago, Detroit, Miami, Boston, Charlotte. These cities, and others, are internationalizing. San Diego, Los Angeles, Las Vegas, Phoenix, San Antonio, Dallas, Austin. These cities are changing rapidly and will continue to change.

And Christianity is a vanguard, helping these people adjust to their new home. As Christians we *should* be cheering for these folks to succeed and thrive in their new home, just as our ancestors did in times past. As Christians, we should be defined more by what we're *for* rather than for what we're *against*.

Many immigrants to the U.S. are Christians. However, many others are not. We are not going to reach them with the good news if they get the impression we're against them, don't want them here, and don't trust them. The only way we are going to impact them for Christ is by letting them know we are on their side. We care about their health, we want their children to thrive, and, indeed, we would love to partner with them in building up the kingdom of God. It is easy to tell whether someone approves of you or is suspicious of you. It is our job, as Christians, to extend a gracious hand to the newcomers in our communities, a hand that they can trust.

Christianity is a force for good in the world, offering so much to the person who will receive its gifts. But as our nation changes demographically and culturally, Christians also need to adapt well. The truth is that Christianity has always excelled in this capacity. That's why it is the largest and most widespread faith in human history. It has assimilated to global cultures in profoundly creative ways. This is an aspect of Christianity we can be proud of.

At the end of our Saddleback visit, my wife and I were trying to round up our four children. They were thoroughly enjoying the place. They loved the live music. They rolled around in the grass. They played on the playground equipment with their new friends. Several times I had to get their attention to let them know it was time to go. It was getting late.

But they didn't want to leave. They were drawn to the church. Being there felt good to them. They had so many reasons to stay.

I cannot think of a better analogy for the church. Church should be a place that we don't want to leave. An effective church is one where people feel safe. They enjoy it. They want to stay. If Christianity lives up to its full potential—if *Christians* live up to their full potential—then we will build something that attracts people. They will feel our acceptance, like my kids felt that evening at Saddleback.

Globally, Christianity is thriving. It is a joy to see. We in the Western world now have millions of brothers and sisters all across the globe in places we've never heard of. And some of them have come our way. The Scriptures tell us they're part of our family. Let's get out there and get to know them.